SPIRITUAL WRITERS OF THE
MIDDLE AGES

IS VOLUME

40

OF THE

Twentieth Century Encyclopedia of Catholicism

UNDER SECTION

IV

THE MEANS OF REDEMPTION

IT IS ALSO THE

71ST

VOLUME IN ORDER OF PUBLICATION

Edited by HENRI DANIEL-ROPS *of the Académie Française*

SPIRITUAL WRITERS
OF THE MIDDLE AGES

By GERARD SITWELL, O.S.B.

HAWTHORN BOOKS · PUBLISHERS · *New York*

First Edition, September, 1961
Second Printing, April, 1964

NIHIL OBSTAT

Carolus Davis, S.T.L.

> *Censor Deputatus*

IMPRIMATUR

E. Morrogh Bernard

> *Vicarius Generalis*

Westmonasterii, die VII JULII, MCMLXI

H-9504

CONTENTS

INTRODUCTION

MEDIEVAL SPIRITUALITY

It will be well to define at the outset the limits within which
the term medieval in the title of this book is being used.
There can be no hard and fast dividing line between one
age and another, but I propose to take the year 1000 as mark-
ing roughly the time when the Middle Ages may be said to
have begun. The Norse invasions, which had disrupted the
Carolingian Empire before it had well got under way,
ceased with the establishment of the Norsemen in Normandy
in the early tenth century, and a hundred years later these
people were taking their place as the most virile and con-
structive of the nations of Europe. This was the period when
North-west Europe was coming to the fore both politically
and intellectually, and it is with the spiritual literature of that
area that we shall be concerned. By the year 1500 the
Renaissance had established itself in the North, and it is not
proposed to take this study of the history of spirituality beyond the end of the fifteenth century.

As it will be used in this book spirituality means in effect
that branch of Christian theology which deals with man's
relation to God in all its aspects. It is a science at once
practical and theoretical, and the name *spiritalis scientia* was
given to it in early days, though it has dropped out of use
now. We can, of course, only study this science historically
in the writings on the subject left by succeeding ages. The
early and medieval literature in which it is enshrined is very
extensive, but it is only in comparatively recent times, the
last fifty years or so, that any serious attempt has been made

to study it. The men of the Counter-Reformation had new and urgent problems in leading the devout life, and they had a highly developed instrument—Spiritual Exercises and their derivative, methodical meditation—to aid them in their task. The spiritual writings of the Fathers and the Middle Ages, approached in a quite unhistorical way, did not seem to offer them or those who came after them what they wanted. Certain principles of Christian behaviour were easily recognized, but the circumstances and mentality of the writers differed so much from those of the post-Tridentine world that their writings appeared almost unintelligible, and those who approached this literature from a practical point of view with the object of deriving help for the individual spiritual life were often disappointed. Today we are becoming conscious of new needs, and the methods of the last three hundred years do not entirely satisfy us. Many are looking back to the older spiritual literature seeking to find in it nourishment for their own spiritual lives, and this is as it should be. The object of the writers was always practical, to lead souls to God. But we shall not find that the nourishment offered us by the spiritual writers of the Middle Ages is predigested. It requires a serious effort to master the idiom in which it is expressed.

The present work deals with a period in which many of the best minds were intensely interested in the study of spirituality, and it may be felt that undue attention has been paid to names hitherto almost or quite unknown, while great names have been left out or received the barest mention. But in treating so large and complex a subject in so small a space it seemed better to point out a few broad movements, rather than to give a catalogue of the vast number of individual writers in the period with a short description of each, and in the matter of spirituality it seemed in some cases that it was the lesser rather than the greater figures who best represented their age.

A great deal has been written on patristic and medieval

spirituality in recent years, particularly in French, but much of/it is scattered in learned journals. If rather more references have been given than is usual in this series, that is because much of the work on which this book is based is very little known, but only a minimum of references has been given, and there is no pretence to a complete bibliography. It is hoped nevertheless that anyone wishing to pursue the subject further will find an opening into various lines of thought. In emphasizing certain main themes, which it is believed give a true picture, many nuances have had to be ignored, but there seemed no alternative in the space available.

CHAPTER I

THE BACKGROUND

EGYPTIAN MONASTICISM

It will help us, and is indeed necessary in order to understand the spiritual writings of the Middle Ages, to know something of what went before. In this respect our date of 1000 is very arbitrary. We are beginning in the middle of a tradition, what was in fact the monastic tradition. We are concerned with the more or less intensive cult of the Christian life and this was not something which began in the Middle Ages. From very early in the Church's history, and it may be presumed from apostolic times, there had been an *élite*, both men and women, ascetics and the virgins as they were called, who sought to lead the life of the Gospel counsels, abstaining from marriage and exercising themselves in fasting and prayer. But they did this as private individuals living in their own homes.[1] It would seem that it was a group of such who, about the year 270, compelled St Anthony to come out from solitude and rule over them, and in this way the manner of life which came to be called monasticism began. The movement grew rapidly and soon came to embrace great numbers, some, loosely organized, living eremitic or quasi-eremitic lives, some under Pachomius living the cenobitical life in communities. The motive was always a more or less literal interpretation of the Gospel invitation which inspired St Antony, "If thou hast a mind to be perfect, go home and sell all that belongs to thee ... then come back and follow

[1] Viller-Rahner, *Ascese und Mystik in der Väterzeit,* pp. 43–9.

me" (Matt. 19. 21). In the beginning at any rate there was no formal ceremony of initiation or taking of vows, but in effect the life embraced by the early monks was the life of poverty, chastity and obedience later consecrated by the three vows of religion. The poverty was extreme, the ideal of obedience far-reaching, though in practice the loose organization even of the cenobites left much scope for individuality. Once launched in Egypt the movement quickly spread to Palestine and Syria, and then to Italy and France, but for long it remained very unorganized, dependent on the personality of local leaders. The early monks were not for the most part intellectuals, far from it,[2] but the capital of the region in which most of them lived was Alexandria, where the last flowering of Greek philosophy was providing the stimulus for the first great theologians of the early Church.

In order to understand the impact this had on monasticism it is necessary to realize that to the intellectuals of Alexandria at the time the large-scale flight to the desert was not so strange a thing as it appears perhaps to us, for two ideas taking their origin from the current Neo-Platonic philosophy and applied to Christianity permeated their thought. There was first of all the idea of a Christian *gnosis*, an illumination of the soul by the Holy Spirit, leading to a high degree of union with God.[3] The Alexandrian Fathers used in fact the term deification, a term which, understood as they understood it, subsequent theology has not failed to endorse. There was further the idea of contemplation and the contemplative life.[4] The motive power behind it was the conviction that there is a real assimilation of the knower to the thing known, so that if the soul is attached through the passions to the material

---

[2] See Cassian, *Conf.*, X, 3. In the year 399 there was a split among the Egyptian monks between those who accepted a more theological approach to spirituality and those who did not. This chapter in Cassian is a reference to it, but he gives a very one-sided, not to say misleading, account. It went much deeper than he suggests.

[3] See Congar, *Dict. Théologie*, t. XV, 1, col. 344.

[4] See "Le Traité de l'Oraison d'Evagre le Pontique", by I. Hausherr, in *Revue Ascétique et Mystique*, 1934, p. 82.

world, it becomes, as it were, coarsened so that it can no longer appreciate the immaterial, it can no longer "see" spiritual things. In the same way in so far as it comes to know the simple and immutable nature of God, it becomes itself simple and immutable. Man's whole end must be to escape from the multiplicity of creatures, that is to say from the movement, change, possibility of growth and diminution, that exists in them, in order to assimilate himself to the Godhead, whose goodness consists precisely in its immutability. This involved, of course, a complete turning away from all creatures (*praxis*) which was to lead to complete indifference to them, a complete freedom from the passions (*apatheia*), so leaving the road open to the contemplation of God. Such in essence was the theory evolved by Evagrius[5] basing himself on Origen, and translated into the terms practical life, purity of heart, and contemplation.

These ideas, of a life in some way divinely illumined, and of a life devoted to the contemplation of God, were familiar to intellectual Christians from their acquaintance with current Greek philosophy, and they had no difficulty in christianizing them. They were not strict alternatives, they were complementary and in fact interacted in various ways. But for the moment it is enough to draw attention to the idea of the contemplative life. Already in the fourth century the Greek Fathers—using the term to cover all Greek-speaking—had analysed the various stages through which the soul passed on its way to the highest union with God. Here the term contemplation is used in a wide sense to describe the activity of a soul occupied so far as possible exclusively with God. The degree of union attained is, of course, impossible to determine, and in any case it will have varied.

[5] In the sixth century the work of Origen became largely discredited owing to certain unorthodox elements which it contained, and it was his connection with Origen which no doubt led to the eclipse of Evagrius. For long his works were thought to have been lost, but modern scholarship has recovered most of them. See O. Chadwick, *John Cassian*, pp. 82–3. It is Evagrius who lies behind the teaching of Cassian.

CASSIAN

A theory of the spiritual life, then, in which the attainment of contemplation played a prominent part, developed in the lands of the eastern Mediterranean, and the knowledge of it was brought to the West by Cassian. Born between 355 and 365, probably in the Dobrudja, he became about 380 a monk at Bethlehem. About six years later he received permission to visit the monks of Egypt, and he remained there probably till 399, when he went to Constantinople and became the disciple of St John Chrysostom. When Chrysostom went into exile in 405, Cassian went to Rome, and perhaps about the year 410 to Marseilles. Here he founded two monasteries, one for women and one for men, but he did not introduce monasticism to this part of the world, for it had already spread to southern Gaul from Egypt. It lacked, however, any firm guidance, and Cassian was asked by a neighbouring bishop to write an account of the Egyptian monasticism, which he had known at first hand. He performed his task in two works, the *Institutes*, in twelve books, and the *Conferences* or *Collations* in twenty-four.

The merest summary of Cassian's teaching can be given here. He divides the spiritual life into two parts, the *actual* or *practical*, and the *theoretic* or *contemplative* (Conf. XIV, 1). The practical life in its turn has two parts, a negative and a positive (*ibid.*, 3). The negative consists in the correction of faults, the positive in the acquirement and practice of virtues. The work of the *actual* life is, of course, the fundamental business of any serious religious endeavour. In some respects Cassian's teaching on it reflects the particular circumstances and ideas of his time, but the basic principles of ascetic training, which have been drawn out and elaborated by a host of writers in succeeding centuries down to our own day, are to be found in Cassian. In particular he recognized that external practices were not ends in themselves, but were means to bring about the perfection of charity. Thus the monk must not be angry if by accident some good work interferes with his customary discipline, "For the gain from fasting will not balance the loss from anger, nor is the profit from reading so great as the harm which results from despising a brother" (Conf. I, 7). The purity of heart at which the monk must aim is something very close to the Greek philosophers' *apatheia*, complete escape from the passions, but it is not quite the same. It is control of the passions not the absence of them that constitutes the Christian's good. Cassian is insistent that temptation will continue, and recognizes in a chapter of great spiritual wisdom (Conf. XVIII, 13) that patience will only come as the result of humility, and that neither of them can be practised except in adversity. If the spiritual life is of necessity a combat, then temptation is not to be deplored, but rather welcomed as a means of proving our love for God (Conf. IX, 23; cf. V, 6, and XXII, 10). It is to be noted that Cassian's *actual* life was a moral training, and in itself had nothing to do with the way a man occupied himself. It was compatible with a life of active good works, but it did not in itself imply the performance of these. It is important, therefore, not to confuse it with the term *active* life, which in the West always carried the idea of good works performed for one's neighbour.

But beyond this life of moral endeavour there was the contemplative life. Cassian speaks (Conf. III, 6) of three renunciations to be made by the monk. The first is that of worldly goods and wealth, the basic renunciation of leaving the world; the second is that "by which we reject the fashions and vices and former affections of soul and flesh", the specific work of the *actual* life; "the third, that by which we detach our soul from all present and visible things, and contemplate only things to come, and set our heart on what is invisible". It is important to realize that he meant by that no less than an ideal of, so far as possible, continuous contemplation. That this is so appears quite clearly from a number of places. In Conference X, chapter 7, he says:

> This then ought to be the aim and purpose of the solitary ... that it may be vouchsafed to him to possess even in the body an image of future bliss, and that he may begin in this world to have a foretaste or a sort of earnest of that celestial life and glory. This, I say, is the end of all perfection, that the mind purged from all carnal desires may daily be lifted towards spiritual things, until the whole life and all thoughts of the heart become one continuous prayer.

He recognized that the ideal was strictly unattainable, but nevertheless it must be striven for.

> To cling to God continually, and to be joined to him inseparably in contemplation is impossible for a man while he is still in this weak flesh of ours. But we ought to be aware on what we should have the purpose of our mind fixed, and to what goal we should ever recall the gaze of our soul; and when the mind can secure this it may rejoice; and grieve and sigh when it is withdrawn from this, and as often as it discovers itself to have fallen away from gazing on him, it should admit that it has lapsed from the highest good, considering that even a momentary departure from contemplation of Christ is fornication. (Conf. I, 13, cf. XIV, 11.)

Again, Conference XXIII brings out very interestingly this ideal of continuous occupation of the mind with God. The Conference is on "Willing the Good and acting evilly" and the discussion is on St Paul's words "For the good which I will I do not, but the evil which I will not that I do" (Rom. 7. 19), and the abbot Theonas, who conducts the discussion, interprets "the evil which I will not that I do" precisely of the inability to keep the mind always occupied with the thought of God (see particularly chapters 4 and 5). It is a surprising interpretation to us, but it shows the value which was attached to this ideal. The conflict which may arise between the ideal of keeping the mind continually on God and the claims of charity is put forward explicitly, and Cassian's attitude is not left in doubt by an anecdote he quotes

(Conf. XXIV, 13). The abbot Macarius illustrates the point he is making by a parable of a barber, who left the city in which he was working to go to another in which he heard that barbers earned more money, but when he got to the other city, he found that the cost of living was so much greater that he was no better off but rather the poorer, and the moral was that it was better to remain in the desert and be sure of what spiritual profits you could get from prayer than work for the conversion of even many souls and become absorbed by distractions. And there is the story of the monk who, when he was asked to extricate an ox which had become bogged down in a swamp, replied that he was unable to do so, because he had been dead for the last twenty years, metaphorically (Conf. XXIV, 9). Cassian does not condemn his attitude, although it is at variance with his own earlier teaching.[6]

For Cassian, then, the ideal at least for the hermit was a life of almost continuous prayer, and of prayer which might frequently be of such intensity as to make it ecstatic.[7] And the background of this spiritual activity was to be a life in which human relationships were to be reduced to a minimum and the least possible thought taken for the needs of the body. The life of the hermit was to be an anticipation of heaven. The claim is often made explicitly. In heaven man will pass from practical works to the love of God and the contemplation of heavenly things, and those who make it their business to obtain purity of heart give themselves "while they are still in the flesh to that duty in which they are to continue, when

[6] See page 15 above.
[7] The abbot John, who had come back from the desert to a monastery, describes the ecstasies he used to experience. "And my soul was so filled with divine meditations and spiritual contemplations that often in the evening I did not know whether I had taken any food, and on the next day was very doubtful whether I had broken my fast the day before" (Conf. XIX, 4). I refer to this view of the contemplative life as Cassian's because there is no doubt that for him it was the ideal and he brought the fullest knowledge of it to the West, but of course it did not originate with him. He reported it as he found it in Egypt. He has also much to say about the cenobitic life, and St Benedict's indebtedness to him is unquestionable.

they have laid aside corruption" (Conf. I, 10). Of the abbot Paphnutius it was said that "he enjoyed and delighted in the daily society of angels" (Conf. III, 1), and the idea that the monastic life was the counterpart on earth of the life of the angels in heaven came to be widespread. In so far as it is the primary duty of a monk to sing the praises of God the comparison of the monastic choir to the angelic choir was natural enough and easily capable of a suitable adaptation, but it was the hermit who was compared to the angel, and the identification of rôles was pushed very far.

The cenobitic life, which existed in Egypt, was of course known to Cassian and he has a good deal to say about it, but there is no doubt that for him the ideal was the hermit's life of continuous contemplation, and it is not difficult to see the influence of Greek thought. Contemplation of God is the good to which everything else must give place, "because there is nothing of itself enduring, nothing unchangeable, nothing good but deity alone" (Conf. XXIII, 3). That is in the pure Greek tradition. Of course for Cassian and the Fathers whose teaching he reproduced the ideal was christianized and immeasurably deepened. The attempt of the Greek philosophers to find God had been a form of escapism, an attempt to side-step the suffering of life and to find happiness in repose. Christianity sought happiness through suffering, man was saved by the passion and death of Christ on the cross. The whole great mystery of suffering and evil was not solved here, because it remains the greatest of mysteries, but sublimated, and resolved only in the paradox that he who loses his life for Christ's sake shall find it. All this lay behind Cassian, but there was in him nevertheless this strong bent towards contemplative union with the One. It was fitted into the Christian tradition, but it did not represent the whole of that tradition.[8]

[8] The idea of continuous contemplation may seem unreal to us in the West, but Cassian's ideal is embodied as perfectly as it can be in the life of staretz Silouan (1866–1938). See *The Undistorted Image* by Archimandrite Sofrony, translated from the Russian by Rosemary Edmonds, London, 1958.

ST BENEDICT

Cassian had brought to the West much information about the monastic life as lived in Egypt, the cenobitical as well as the eremitical, but it cannot be said that he gave any firm guidance. He said too much, and it was not till nearly a hundred years later that St Benedict provided a pattern to which in the end the whole of Western monasticism would more or less exactly conform. St Benedict knew the works of Cassian and revered them, but he legislated for cenobites. Granted the unorganized and indeed disorderly state of monasticism in his day it was perhaps inevitable that he should have done so. The condition of monasticism in the West at that time is well illustrated by St Benedict's own early experience. He left Rome as a student, disgusted with the evil and corruption he found there. We do not know how old he was, but he must have been a very young man, perhaps only a boy of seventeen, and he became a hermit. A monk called Romanus used to lower bread to him in a basket over the cliff face above his hermitage, but St Gregory does not tell us that he did anything else for him. The outcome of his self-training in the solitary life was a success, a fact which we can only attribute to the grace of God working in a character which must have had great strength and poise. Humanly speaking his experiment might have ended disastrously. After he had converted some rough shepherds in the neighbourhood, and evidently acquired a reputation, the monks of a nearby monastery asked him to rule over them, but their quality is shown by the fact that when they found his rule too strict for their liking they tried to poison him. When he came to write his *Rule* he described four kinds of monks (chap. I), and two of them, the sarabaites and gyrovagues, were wholly unsatisfactory. It is true that most of his description comes from Cassian, but there is no reason why St Benedict should have quoted it, if it had not been relevant to the Italy of his day. We may well believe that St Benedict's experience had convinced him that, unless a firm foundation is first provided by exercise in the discipline of the *actual* life, the overcoming of faults and the practice of virtue, no form of monasticism is likely to be a success. Cassian had recognized that this foundation was better attained among cenobites than in the individualistic life of the hermit, and this was certainly St Benedict's opinion when he came to write his *Rule*. He speaks of the eremitical life with respect, but he says that it is for those who "after long probation in a monastery, having learnt in association with many brethren how to fight against the devil, go out well armed from the ranks of the community to the solitary combat of the desert" (chap. I).

The ideal of continuous contemplation was recognized by Cassian as being only attainable—in so far as it was attainable —by hermits, and St Benedict wrote a rule for cenobites, and in time though not immediately, in one form or another, it became practically the universal rule for monks in the West, and the break with Cassian's extreme contemplative tradition would seem to have been complete. In this connection it is to be noted that when St Benedict speaks of monks going out from the monastery to become hermits, he does not say anything about contemplation. He speaks of them as having learnt to fight against the devil, and as going out well armed to the "solitary combat of the desert". That was a prominent feature in Cassian's presentation of monasticism, and it owed something perhaps to the Greek conception of the struggle between flesh and spirit, but it had after all its roots in the New Testament, in St Paul—"our wrestling is not with flesh and blood but with spiritual wickedness in high places" (Ephes. 6. 12, Douay)—and in the Gospels. But for Cassian the achievement of contemplation was the real aim, and St Benedict does not mention the word in his *Rule*.

Nevertheless St Benedict left room for it. A considerable part of his monks' day was spent in *lectio divina*. We shall see much of this later, and here we need only note that in the early Church it was the foundation of both theology and spirituality—indeed the two were hardly distinguished. It was here that the enlightenment by the Holy Spirit played its part, the Christian *gnosis*. Scripture was the Word of God, and it was only under the influence of the Holy Ghost that its true spiritual meaning could be grasped—this was the particular Alexandrian contribution, and it was never altogether lost sight of in the Middle Ages. To read Scripture was in fact to meditate on it, and the process could very easily turn into prayer, and a prayer which could become fully contemplative. Cassian shows us (Conf. X, 11) how the prayer of the Fathers of the desert was based on the psalms, and how what we should recognize as a fully contemplative prayer could arise from the meditative assimilation of them. But the crucial point is that for St Benedict perfection does not consist in tranquillity and contemplation but in charity. Cassian recognized the pre-eminence of charity, but he identified it with purity of heart (Conf. I, 5), and he comes very near to identifying this with *apatheia*; "though still in this corruptible flesh they (hermits) seek that state which they will find when they lay aside their corruption, and attain to the promise of our Lord and Saviour: 'Blessed are the pure in heart for they shall see God' " (Conf. I, 10). It is the conscious striving after the angelic life. St Benedict would lead his monks to perfection, to that perfect charity which casts out fear (chap. VII), but it was a perfection which was to consist in the perfection of humility and obedience. If contemplation follows it is the work of God. It is unlikely that he did not see the possibility, it seems certain that he experienced the reality, but he would wait for it to come.

CHAPTER II

SPIRITUALITY FROM THE ELEVENTH TO THE FOURTEENTH CENTURY

ELEVENTH-CENTURY BENEDICTINE SPIRITUALITY

Two elements, we have seen, contributed to the "spiritual science" as first developed by the Alexandrian Fathers. There was first the ever-increasing realization of the divine mysteries as revealed in Scripture under the influence of the Holy Spirit, and there was the idea of the contemplative life, the effort to conform the soul to the simplicity of God, an effort which demanded withdrawal from the world, and even, as far as might be, from human relationships of any kind.

In Egyptian monasticism the second of these, the contemplative idea, came to overshadow the other element and practically to exclude it. But this extreme view of contemplation was not taken up in the West. St Benedict legislated for a life with which it was not compatible, but, though he does not directly mention contemplation in his *Rule*, he left open, as we have seen, a way by which the other method of attaining it might come in. And this is in fact what happened.

All theology is reflection on revealed mysteries, and for the Greek Fathers, who were laying the foundations, this meant meditation on Scripture, a gradual drawing out and realization of the meaning, but with little speculation in the scholastic sense. It was an unfolding of the Faith under the influence of God. This was the great Patristic tradition, and the monks in their measure adhered to it. The spirituality of the early Middle Ages was necessarily that of the cloisters, for it had developed in the Dark Ages, when conditions were such that civilized life hardly existed elsewhere, and the life led in the monasteries, when conditions were favourable— and this was far from always being the case—was one of great simplicity and recollection, and it was one which was inspired by a high ideal, the ideal which in the increasing number of monasteries which followed the Benedictine *Rule* was embodied in the instruction to find out whether the novice truly seeks God. This was the single purpose of the fervent, and it was one to which their life permitted them to devote themselves in a very direct and literal way. From as early as the time of Charles the Great the manual labour of primitive days had largely dropped out, and the monk's time was divided principally between the liturgy and reading. The liturgy was the direct service of God, and the matter of the reading consisted almost exclusively of the Scriptures and certain of the Fathers. Thus the greater part of the day was directly related to God, and there is no question but that the driving force in their lives was a very real desire to attain to God. They desired to know him in some way directly, to make his mysteries real, to bring them home to themselves, and in order to achieve this they meditated upon what they read. We have to be very careful of our terminology here. For us meditation in a religious context has come to mean something very methodical and consisting primarily of ratiocination, an exercise of the reason on religious truth. For the medieval monks it may be that their reading of texts produced something that we should rather call contemplation, but in the natural sense of the word. They contemplated revealed truth as they found it in the Scriptures or the Fathers much as an artist might contemplate a picture. But there was, of course, an affective element, an element of love accompanying and vivifying the experience. That the grace of God might, as it were, take hold, and that their contemplation might become something God-given, a partial withdrawal of the veils covering the divine truth, was something of which they were very well aware. It was something which they did not expect to happen at all frequently, and which they did not expect to be of long duration, but it was something which was known to some of them at least by experience. The Greek Fathers had analysed the process and given it a theological background. They had established the fact, later accepted into mystical theology, that in its fullest sense it was a direct communication with God which necessarily exceeded the natural powers of the soul to receive. It was contemplation "without means", without any intermediary of the action of the natural powers. That was one way of expressing it which we shall meet. It was also described by saying that the union in love and knowledge with God took place above or beyond the intellect, in the "fine point" of the soul. The monks of the Dark and early Middle Ages knew the descriptions left by Augustine and Gregory, but they had little or no speculative knowledge about it. When they used the word contemplation they always included a wider sense of simply a God-given knowledge and love which exceeded ordinary experience but was within the normal capacity of the powers of the soul raised by grace to receive. For a history of mysticism in the strict sense the distinction would be important. Here it is not. Their lives were certainly contemplative in a wide sense of the word, but what they cultivated was not this extreme experience but a meditative consideration of the mysteries of faith, and this might lead to a knowledge and love of God which was certainly infused, if not mystical in the full sense mentioned above. Their immediate master in this type of theology was, of course, Augustine. For him theology meant just this progressive insight into the great mysteries of faith under the influence of the Holy Spirit. The unimpeded vision of God, which constitutes the fullness of man's beatitude, is attained only in heaven, but here on earth man may attain an ever-increasing illumination of which the culminating point is contemplation, the effect of the gift of Wisdom.[1] And if the great name of Augustine finds little mention in this book, it must not be forgotten that it is he who lies behind this search of the monks for the experience of God. St Bernard, who saw the beginnings of scholasticism, recognized the place of and the need for a scientific, objective, knowledge of God, but he distinguishes this from the other, subjective, knowledge, which is the result of the gift of wisdom in us (Cant. XXIII, 14).

JOHN OF FÉCAMP

With these general ideas in mind we may examine some of the writings which are representative of this spirituality, and we may begin with John of Fécamp. He was born about the year 990 in the neighbourhood of Ravenna and in his youth became a monk in the abbey of Fruttuaria, where his uncle, Blessed William of Volpiano, was abbot. It was the period when Europe was settling down after the disruption caused by the last of the barbarian invasions, that of the Norsemen, and the vitality of the Christian religion was manifesting itself in a series of reforms of the monastic life, and was soon to show itself in the great general reforms associated with the name of Gregory VII. Cluny had shown the way, but many followed its lead, and William of Volpiano among them. Starting from North Italy his influence extended through Burgundy and Lorraine as far as Normandy. John went with his uncle from Fruttuaria to the foundation of the abbey of St Benignus at Dijon, and then in the year 1017 was made prior of Fécamp, at no great distance from Bec in Normandy.

[1] See M.-J. Congar in the *Dictionnaire de théologie catholique*, t. XV, col. 350–53, and for a fuller treatment E. Gilson's *Introduction à l'étude de Saint Augustin*. It is virtually the theme of the whole book. Cf also Plagnieux, *Saint Grégoire de Nazianze Théologien*, especially chapter III.

In 1028 he became abbot of Fécamp and remained so till his death fifty years later in 1078. From 1054 he was also abbot of St Benignus at Dijon, and Fécamp before his death had become the head of a congregation or federation of abbeys. Such briefly are the facts of his life. Feudalism was at its height, and abbots as big landowners played an important rôle in the feudal hierarchy, so that John was necessarily much engaged in public affairs, his connections with North Italy even bringing him into contact with the Empire. It is well to remember this background to the evidently intense spiritual life which he led.

But it is with his writings rather than with his public life that we are concerned, and the history of these is curious in the extreme. For centuries they disappeared from view entirely as the work of John, for, although most of them got into print when the big folio editions of the Fathers appeared in the sixteenth and seventeenth centuries, they sheltered under such famous names as Augustine and Anselm. It was Dom André Wilmart who by going back to the manuscripts was able to disinter the work of John and restore to him a respectable *corpus* of writings.[2] It is thus only in the last thirty years or so that he has been put on the map as an important spiritual author of the early Middle Ages.

The writings of John of Fécamp illustrate perfectly the spirituality which grew out of *lectio divina*. They consist essentially in the sort of affective prayer to which this gave rise, incorporating much of the text, and at the same time expounding it and growing out of it. Sometimes the expressions of love appear spontaneous, sometimes, and more generally, motivated by the considerations in the text. His most important work is the *Confessio Theologica*. Made primarily for his own use, he calls it a *defloratiuncula*, a little posy, and it has indeed many quotations from the Scriptures,

[2] See Dom Wilmart's *Auteurs Spirituels*, pp. 126–37, and 173–201. Dom Jean Leclercq has published the most important of John's texts together with some unknown to Wilmart in his *Jean de Fécamp* (Paris, 1946).

the liturgy and certain of the Fathers; almost entirely Augustine, Gregory and Alcuin. But it is much more than an
arbitrary collection of texts. It has a theme, even if it is
only loosely put together. The first part treats of the divinity
of the Father, the Son and the Holy Ghost; the second of the
graces of the Redemption, and the necessity for faith and
good works; the third of the desire for Christ and sorrow
for sin. John has collected texts on these subjects, but the
quotations, which in any case form less than half of the work,
are woven together into the form of a continuous prayer, and
this at once gives the character of the piece. He is not concerned to argue or explain, but to adore; the consideration of
the texts he brings forward has simply led to prayer. The
title suggests the *Confessions* of Augustine, and that he had
the famous book in mind is evinced by the fact that almost
at the beginning he quotes a passage from Augustine's *Confessions* which runs to fifty lines in Leclercq's edition, and
there are many more, but he uses the word in the sense of a
Confession of praise, as indeed did Augustine.[3] But it is not
John's purpose to relate his spiritual development, and he
thanks God that his life had involved no great crisis of conversion. The passages he takes from Augustine are always
those in which God is addressed directly. It is God and the
relation of his soul to God here and now which interests him.
In the *Confessio Theologica* we find crystallized, as it were,
the results of John of Fécamp's reading, and of great interest
is a passage in the *explicit* of the Third Part, right at the end
of the whole work, which tells us why he had threaded together this collection of texts.

There are many kinds of contemplation in which the soul
devoted to Thee, O Christ, takes its delight, but in none of
these do I so rejoice as in that which, ignoring all things, directs
a simple glance of the untroubled spirit to Thee alone, O God.
What peace and rest and joy does the soul find in Thee then.

[3] See the *Retractions*, Migne, *Patrologia Latina*, 32, 632, hereafter
referred to as *P.L.* followed by volume and column number.

> For while my mind yearns for divine contemplation, and meditates, and expresses Thy glory to the best of its ability, the burden of the flesh weighs less heavily upon it; the tumult of thoughts dies down; the weight of mortality and misery no longer exerts its accustomed pressure; all is silent and tranquil. The heart burns within, the spirit rejoices, the memory grows fresh, the intellect clear, and the whole spirit, on fire with longing for the vision of Thy beauty, sees itself carried away to the love of those things which are invisible. And so it is not from any presumptuous boldness, but from a great longing to feel a desire for Thee that I have made this little posy, so that I might always be able to carry about with me a short manual of the word of God, from the reading of which I might rekindle the flame of my love.

The passage bears witness to the high degree of spirituality which was attained by the black monks of the eleventh century. The whole process is very simple. Quiet, meditative reading occupies the mind with thoughts about God, the thoughts give rise to acts, to affective prayer, and this may become simplified till it merges into a prayer which is contemplative.

In the *Letter to a Nun*[4] we have a more objective exposition of John's conception of the spiritual life. He begins by making a series of demands that are very reminiscent of, and sometimes actually incorporate, St Benedict's instruments of good works (*Rule*, chap. 4). This is the ascetic training which is the necessary basis of any spiritual life. But his nun has chosen Mary's part, and it is in order to help her in this that he asks her to accept the handful of sweet flowers that he has collected, evidently a *defloratio* such as the *Confessio Theologica* that he made for himself, but this other has not survived. The book is to play the same part for her that his own played for him, and he encourages her to make use of it with humility and love. "Rise up, then, devoted soul ... that you may drink from the fountain of heavenly

---

[4] Printed by Leclercq, *op. cit.*, p. 205. The title is editorial and descriptive. Nothing is known of the original recipient.

sweetness, saying with the prophet, For with Thee is the fountain of life, and in Thy light we shall see light" (Psalm 35. 10). And he heaps up Scriptural texts in the same sense from the psalms and the Canticle of Canticles. That it is a high degree of contemplation which he expects his nun to attain on occasion is clear from the fact that he warns her against thinking that she may have had experience of the divine Essence as it is in itself. It is only in the next world that we look for this, and whatever experience we have of God now will be fleeting and of short duration. He stresses that the soul drawn up to these heights cannot long remain there.

He then goes on to say (section X) that there are some souls so drawn to the cultivation of this experience that they have little taste for anything else. The occupation of Martha, which he had described as good and necessary, does not benefit them, and it is not to be forced upon them. But, he goes on, there are others, and they are the strongest sort of souls, who "acting with moderation and discretion conform themselves to the lives of both Martha and Mary, and at the King's command sacrifice themselves under the yoke of obedience even in their good desires". He ends up by committing her to God, that under his guidance she may advance in both lives, now with Martha occupied, but temperately, in good deeds, now with Mary resting in the Word of God, *verbo Dei vacans*. The passage illustrates very clearly the Benedictine influence in this spirituality. John recognizes a purely contemplative vocation, as St Benedict did, that of the hermits, who were never entirely lacking in the West—it is possible that he had a certain yearning after it himself[5]— but he states clearly here that it is better to sacrifice even such a desire under the yoke of obedience, and to conform

---

[5] The short *Lamentation* (printed by Leclercq, p. 184), which is an ardent and eloquent aspiration after the hidden life with God, suggests this. How far it represents what he felt, and how far what he would like to have felt, it is difficult to decide. On the *Lamentation* see Leclercq, *Jean de Fécamp*, pp. 46–50.

oneself to the lives of both Martha and Mary.[6] St Benedict's contribution to monastic history came precisely from the fact that he regarded the cenobites as, in the words of the Rule, "the strongest sort of monks" (Chap. I), and John will not go back on the cenobitic ideal, but we have seen that the basis of the nun's spiritual life is to be the practice of what are in effect St Benedict's instruments of good works. The result of this for Benedict was to be humility leading to charity, the perfect love of God which casts out fear, and from there the door to contemplation is open.

Another work by John, the *Confessio Fidei*,[7] which is substantially of the same type as the *Confessio Theologica* and is indeed partly a rehandling of it, illustrates very well how this monastic approach to theology was of itself a spiritual one, and led quite naturally to a life of prayer and union with God. The opening section brings out the character of the whole work and the attitude of mind in which it was conceived. After invoking the Holy Spirit, the true light, he asserts that God has led him to a certain relish of the faith.

O my God, with modest knowledge and sweet love, my faith, which thou hast led forth from darkness to the perception of truth, calls on thee; the faith, sweet as honey, which thou gavest me, when the bitterness of the world had been replaced by the sweetness of charity. [And this faith, not dry but full of spiritual sweetness, drives him to the praise of God:] How sweet it has become in the mouth of my heart, how sweet to the very palate of my spirit! How strongly and persistently it beats on my mind, and moves it, admonishing my whole spirit that it should take its delight in praising thee ... so that my heart may glow in praise of thy glory and my soul pant after thee, my mind burn with thy love, forgetful of vanity and

---

[6] The reminiscences of the *Rule* are manifest, though of course not surprising. St Benedict calls discretion "the mother of the virtues" (chap. 64), and the emphasis on moderation is marked, e.g. the last paragraph of the Prologue. He speaks of fighting under the true King, Christ (Prol.), and though he does not use the phrase "yoke of obedience", but "yoke of the Rule" (chap. 58), it may be said to be the theme of the Prologue.

[7] Printed under the name of Alcuin, *P.L.*, 101, 1027–1098.

misery, so that looking only on thee, astonished and dumb-founded, it may adhere to thy unchanging glory, and may look on thee, the sun of justice, with the eyes of faith.

It would be a mistake to confuse the feeling he is referring to with the devotion felt in the first fervour of a conversion. Far short of contemplation in the full sense of the word there is a sort of intuitive knowledge of God, which is the result of sanctifying grace strengthening and enlivening both faith and charity. There is an added awareness, an entering into and "tasting" of divine things,[8] though, as we have seen, the experience need not stop there. That is what the consideration of the Trinity, to which his book is chiefly devoted, is to mean for John. He is in no way concerned with harmonizing dogma and human knowledge, or with setting out revealed truth in a systematic manner, but at the same time it would be a mistake to see his work as merely the outcome of a spontaneous and simple piety. We must not forget the intellectual background, apprehended perhaps unconsciously by John, in the traditional approach to Scripture. Behind Augustine, the Greek Fathers had seen the *Logos* as the only adequate expression of the things of God, and man could only attain to these in so far as he could attain to the *Logos* by contemplating him.[9] For Origen Scripture repre-sented, as it were, the accidents of the *Logos*, it was the manifestation of the Word of God in order that it might become the food of the soul. The content of Christian revela-tion was not a matter for debate; it was a mystery to be plumbed not by human ingenuity but by the illumination of the Holy Spirit.[10] The great Carmelite writers of the sixteenth

[8] Cf. Fr Voillaume in *Jesus Caritas* (Jan. 1960), pp. 11 and 12.
[9] See J. Daniélou, *Origen*, pp. 131 ff.
[10] The greatest figure among the Benedictines of the eleventh century was, of course, St Anselm (1033–1109). He made a lasting mark as a speculative theologian, but his piety was of an entirely affective kind, and is illustrated in his *Meditations and Prayers* (Schmitt, III, pp. 3–91). Of all those attributed to him in Migne modern scholarship allows only three Meditations (Nos. II, III, XI) and nineteen Prayers. In a short Prologue Anselm says that the purpose of these writings

century, St Teresa and St John of the Cross, analysed very minutely the stages through which the soul might pass in its relation with God, and since their day these various stages, prayer of quiet, simple union, transforming union and so forth, have become almost textbook terms. This was a refinement quite unknown to the early Middle Ages. What the writers of that age meant by contemplation was the attainment of a simple and loving knowledge of God, which was intuitive, but which was also the fruit of a certain, though limited, personal activity. They assumed that the grace of God was concomitant—they generally called it illumination—but they made no attempt to measure the extent of its influence. We have seen reason to believe that John of Fécamp expected it on occasion to produce a high degree of contemplation, but none of these writers was concerned to attempt any definition of degrees in the process, nor do they provide the evidence to enable us to fit their experience into the later categories.

HERMITS: ST ROMUALD, ST JOHN GUALBERT, ST PETER DAMIAN

Before turning to one other feature of this tradition which should be noticed, a word ought to be said about the eremitic life in Western Europe in the early Middle Ages. It had become firmly implanted before the time of St Benedict, and to the end of the Middle Ages hermits were scattered throughout the countryside from Italy to the North of England; in Italy in the tenth and eleventh centuries a number of attempts were made to organize a form of life which was at least quasi-

---

is to excite the mind of the reader to the love and fear of God, and to the consideration of his own state. They are to be read quietly, slowly, a little at a time, with earnest and deliberate meditation— precisely the conception of the traditional *lectio divina*. If there is a more articulated theological background in some of them than in the writings of John, that is perhaps not surprising in a theologian of Anselm's calibre, but essentially they illustrate perfectly the spirituality we have been considering.

eremitical. St Romuald (950–1027) at Camaldoli and else-where, St John Gualbert (990–1073) at Vallombrosa, and St Peter Damian (1007–72) all established groups of disciples who led lives of great austerity with perpetual silence, strict enclosure and no manual labour. The inspiration of the movement was partly penitential. Before the reforms of Gregory VII in the second half of the eleventh century had checked the demoralization following the barbarian invasions, concubinage, clerical incontinence and simony were widely prevalent, and the lives of all these reformers must be seen partly as a reaction against the morals of their time. The elements of penance and reparation entered largely into their view of the spiritual life, but partly too, of course, the inspiration was simply to lead the contemplative life as it had always been known. They led their lives in great simplicity in the manner of the early Egyptian monks, desirous of cutting themselves off from the world and giving themselves to God. They knew about the example of the old monks and consciously followed it, but they knew little about theories of contemplation. St Gregory of Nyssa on the nature of the soul, for example, would have meant nothing to them. Their world, to put it bluntly, was too little educated. In the twelfth and thirteenth centuries the speculations of the Greek Fathers would again be taken up, and a theological basis supplied to the spiritual life, but at this period there could be no question of that. They used the Fathers and the Scriptures— we must suppose, for they have left us no evidence—in the way that John of Fécamp used them. Their theology was, necessarily, the monastic theology of their day, but they gave themselves to it more exclusively than did the cenobites. These particular attempts to return to the desert produced little beyond local results—which are still discernible—but they had perhaps influence on later efforts of the same sort in northern Europe of which mention will be made.

DEVOTION TO CHRIST

For the moment we may return to the main stream represented by John of Fécamp and note the marked devotion to Christ which characterized it. John's preoccupation was always with the goodness of God, his love and mercy. Most benign, most merciful, most loving, are the sort of epithets he heaps up in addressing him. It is this loving God who is the object of our adoration and our desire, and it is through Christ that we come to him. That is the theme which runs through the second part of the *Confessio Theologica* and is continued in the third.

> The third Part begins in which the soul full of devotion, inspired with ardent love for Christ, yearning and sighing for him, desiring to see him whom alone it loves, finds nothing sweet but lamentation and tears; is attracted to nothing but to flee, to be silent, and to take its rest saying, Who will give me the wings of a dove, and I will fly and be at rest?

The writings of John are certainly Christocentric, but his devotion to Christ is distinguished from that which was to develop later. He is not concerned with the details of his earthly existence, but simply with the Person Christ, God and man, who is our Redeemer.[11] It is through him that John here and now looks to be united with God.[12]

PETER OF CELLE

Another interesting witness to this monastic spirituality is Peter, who became in 1145 abbot of the Benedictine monas-

[11] A prayer on the Symbol of Faith, which might be by John and certainly comes from his *milieu* (Wilmart, *Auteurs Spirituels*, pp. 56–63), has a detailed enumeration of the circumstances of Christ's life. It might be called a sort of blue-print for devotion to the Humanity.

[12] John of Fécamp had disciples and imitators and his own work was widely used; a witness to his influence and to the fact that his type of spirituality was widespread. See "Ecrits Spirituels de l'école de Jean de Fécamp", by Dom Jean Leclercq in *Studia Anselmiana*, (1948), 20, pp. 91–114.

tery of Celle near Troyes.[13] He was later abbot of St Rémy
at Rheims, and in 1181 became bishop of Chartres, but his
tenure of this office was short, for he died in 1183. There
is no doubt of his place in the old tradition, but he was a
contemporary of the early Cistercians and his writings perhaps
show traces of their influence. He was also contemporary with
that flowering of the intellectual life among the secular clerks
which goes by the name of the twelfth-century renaissance,
and it is rather surprising to find a definite link connecting
him with it in the shape of his correspondence with John of
Salisbury, one of its outstanding personalities. Peter figures
as the recipient of many letters from John, and the editor
of a recent edition of these observes, "it is remarkable that
here (letter 112) as elsewhere John's choicest classical subtle-
ties and most elaborate banter were addressed to Peter".[14]
At first sight it is surprising that this cultured, man-of-affairs
cleric should have been on these terms with a Benedictine
abbot of markedly contemplative tendencies, but the explanation is to be found in Peter's evident gift for friendship—
John had stayed at Celle. In the considerable body of his
correspondence are to be found letters to popes, kings and
ecclesiastical dignitaries, including St Thomas of Canterbury,
of a more or less formal nature, but the greater number of
his letters consists of intimate and friendly talks with abbots
and monks and simple priests. He seems to have been in
touch with every known existing Order and Congregation,
Cluniacs, Cistercians, Carthusians and the rest, as well as the
secular clergy. Not in any sense an intellectual—he appears
to have been uninfluenced by the theological speculations of
the school of Chartres, for example—his letters reflect his
religious and even contemplative interests, but he had that
innate sympathy with other people which is the basis of a
real capacity for friendship, and in his letters he had the born

[13] Most of his works are printed in *P.L.*, 202, but several missing
in that collection have been printed by Dom Jean Leclercq in *La
Spiritualité de Pierre de Celle*, Paris, 1946.
[14] C. N. L. Brooke, *The Letters of John of Salisbury*, I, p. 1.

letter-writer's gift of a conversational style. This gift for friendship that he manifested was characteristic of the spiritual writers of his age—one thinks of Bernard and Aelred at once—and that they attached great value to it is shown by the fact that Aelred discussed the subject at length. Nor did he regard it as a concession to human weakness. It was something which was integrated into the spirituality of these men who led austere lives, and it is an attractive feature which is not to be ignored in judging their spirituality.

Apart from his letters Peter of Celle has left a large number of sermons, several treatises on Scripture, and various small works on the monastic life. The considerable number, or at least the length, of his works which draw their inspiration directly from Scripture, is an indication of the place reading the Bible must have taken in his life, and that in itself is in conformity with the tradition of the cloisters. He did not, of course, write commentaries in our sense, he did not seek to explain the text, but he was interested in drawing from it spiritual teaching by means of an allegorical interpretation. Thus the description of the tabernacle given in the book of *Exodus* becomes for him a symbol of the soul as the habitation of God. That is the root idea, but it is enveloped in a mass of allegorical interpretation of detail that makes it very difficult to disentangle. All we need note here is that the very existence of these treatises is a witness to the sort of spirituality we have been describing. It provided the spiritual nourishment the monks were looking for, and the same would be true of the sermons preached to his monks.

His minor works on the monastic life are difficult to assess briefly, and here we can only notice a few points. The spiritual writings of John of Fécamp were entirely unspeculative, and contained very little in the way of practical instructions. They provided matter for meditation, but the method was supposed to be known. The early Cistercian writers, as will be seen, began to supply an outline scheme of the various stages the soul may pass through in its relation with God, and also more in the way of positive instruction. In Peter of Celle, perhaps it could be said, is to be found an adumbration of such a scheme in the little treatise *Of Purity*,[15] and a good deal of instruction given in a rather haphazard and discursive way in the other treatises. To this extent he reflects the tendencies of his time, but far more convincingly he illustrates the way in which meditative reading can give rise to a profound and contemplative spirituality.

Before discussing this we may note that the emphasis on devotion to Christ is greater than in John of Fécamp, but the approach to it is the same. Christ is the good Jesus, seen as God and man, thought of as present. He is considered not in the details of his life on earth, but only in the great acts of his passion and death and resurrection. He is thought of as the Christ living now, who suffered and died and rose again for us. For Peter, as for John, the humanity was never separated from the divinity. Thus in a passage referring to the Eucharist: "To come to Christ is to come to the Lord, to come to the King, to the light, the fire, the bread, the vine, yes, and to life itself. You seek liberty? Come to the Lord. You seek security? Come to the King. . . . Glory? Come to the light. . . . You seek resurrection? Come to that which is life itself"[16]—he is referring to the Eucharist, it is to be remembered. It is by uniting ourselves with Christ on the cross that we can be victorious in our conflict with Satan, and Peter brings out the surely very valuable idea that it is the constant daily discipline of the monastic life which unites us to the passion of Christ. It is in the effort of self-conquest that we find our mortification. So the cloister is the *vicarium crucis*, it provides us with our cross. The monk by the very fact of his monastic life, by his dedication to the *actual* life, is nailed to the cross, "that he may be withheld from evil, but be free for all good".[17]

---

[15] Leclercq, *op. cit.*, pp. 174–92.
[16] *Of Monastic Discipline*, chap. 25; *P.L.*, 202, 1137.
[17] *Of Monastic Discipline*, chap. 6; *P.L.*, 202, 1110.

Peter of Celle refers not infrequently to Christ in the sacrament of the holy Eucharist. One passage has already been quoted, and, to give only a few examples, in one of his sermons consideration of the risen Christ leads him to Christ in the sacrament of the altar. "Let him imitate", he says of the priest, "our Redeemer who redeemed us by his blood, by celebrating Mass, by consecrating the Eucharist . . . for man is born once and once regenerated, but daily in bringing to mind the passion of Christ he dies with him."[18] Again, in his book on the monastic life he envisages the monks for whom he was writing as receiving Communion daily. "Urged on by a holy hunger, he (the monk) is refreshed daily by communion of the Body and Blood of the Lord."[19] Devotion to the Blessed Sacrament in the Middle Ages is an enigma. It is well known that it was not customary to receive Communion frequently; the Cistercian lay-brothers, for example, at this time only received it seven times in the year. But no doubt in this they were equated with laymen in the world, and Peter of Celle was thinking of monks who were priests for whom it would be normal to say Mass daily. For Peter at any rate the life of private prayer is magnificently integrated with the liturgy. It is the same Christ who is to be contemplated in his glory, found in reading (meditation), and received in the sacrament of the holy Eucharist.[20] "O Jesus, whom the Father sent to feed his people, give us our bread, give us thyself, the food of our life. . . . O Lord Jesus, my soul lives only nourished by thee. Nothing but thy body satisfies it."[21] Dom Jean Leclercq has collected an impressive number of texts in which Peter refers to Christ as King,[22] but he is also the Bridegroom of the soul. The image, of course, comes from the Canticle of Canticles. As early as Origen this work had been used to illustrate the relation of the soul to Christ, and

[18] Sermon 35, *P.L.*, 202, 745.
[19] *Of Monastic Discipline*, chap. 25; *P.L.*, 202, 1137.
[20] Letter 47, *P.L.*, 202, 471.
[21] *Of Bread*, chap. 19, *P.L.*, 202, 1012.
[22] *La Spiritualité de Pierre de Celle*, pp. 133–5.

in Peter's own lifetime it provided St Bernard with the inspiration for some of his most famous sermons. Peter based none of his writings explicitly upon it, but with his discursive style the introduction of the theme presented no difficulty.

On the connection between his spirituality and *lectio divina* Peter of Celle is more explicit than John of Fécamp, for he has left a treatise, *Of Mortification and Reading*,[23] dealing with the subject directly. The novice fighting under the banner of Christ, he says, has a threefold discipline to embrace, bodily mortification, by which the unruly motions of the flesh are restrained, reading of the Old and New Testaments, by which the soul is nourished, and prayer, by which it is raised to God. He treats only of the first two, and of these mortification is part of the moral training or discipline which is always demanded as a foundation. His teaching on it, in keeping with this whole tradition, is very moderate. It is to be, he says, a persecution of vice, not of nature; the body is to be corrected as a friend, not hated as an enemy.[24] But he does not dwell long on this, and he passes on to the subject of reading. It is to be the reading of Scripture, very likely presented in the form of selected texts roughly grouped according to subject matter, a *florilegium*, but we know that the Fathers were also read. To use a phrase from one of his letters it is to be *saporabilis lectio*,[25] a tasting of what is read, and is to be distinguished from the reading of scholastic treatises. He is broad-minded about these and does not banish them altogether from his cloisters, but he has no enthusiasm for them, and is of the opinion that they will hinder rather than help the proper work of the monks.[26] The manner of reading which he advocates is really meditation, essentially what we mean by the word, thinking about the content of the text, but sentence by sentence as it comes—something quite removed from

[23] Printed by Leclercq, *op. cit.*, pp. 231–9. The title *De Afflictione et lectione* is Leclercq's. See his note on p. 41.
[24] *Ibid.*, p. 231, 16 and 17.
[25] Letter 28, *P.L.*, 202, 436.
[26] *Of Conscience*, Leclercq, *op. cit.*, p. 238.

the methodical and formal meditation of later times. It is to be a digesting of what is read, and he uses the metaphor freely. "As food is of no value unless it is digested, so reading without meditation is of little benefit . . . reading is valuable when it is followed by assiduous meditation."[27] And he speaks of "reading by which the soul is fed".[28] The real nature of the spiritual reading of the cloisters is disclosed when he tells us that all the questions raised by it are to be reduced to one, the relationship of ourselves to God—in other words the texts are all to be applied to the individual soul. If the psalmist is surrounded by his enemies, it is my soul which is beset with evil tendencies, the journey of the Israelites from Egypt to the Promised Land is the journey of my soul from the bondage of sin to the freedom of heaven. The application of the texts in this way will bring about an intimacy with God, and, equally important, a knowledge of ourselves.[29] Peter is explicit that reading done in this way will lead to contemplation; "from holy reading and meditation there comes the contemplation of heavenly things".[30] The process is the normal one already outlined by Gregory. It begins with recollection. "The Lord teaches in the Gospel how the conscience (conscientia, in the sense rather of consciousness) ought to shut itself up within itself, saying: Enter into your inner room. What is the inner room, if not the secret place of the conscience? What is the door, if not your mouth? When you pray, therefore, enter into the inner room of a tranquil and quiet mind, where the Lord is who dwells in Sion."[31]

The result is rather referred to in a hundred places as something to be taken for granted than formally expounded. The soul is "urged on to seek God, not to discuss him. She seeks to see the face not to define the incomprehensibility of God; she rejoices if she finds what is sufficient for faith; she

[27] Sermon 69, P.L., 202, 857.
[28] Of Mortification, Leclercq, op. cit., p. 231.
[29] Of Mortification, Leclercq, op. cit., p. 231, 235 and cf. p. 67.
[30] Sermon 69, P.L., 202, 857 D.
[31] Of Conscience, Leclercq, op. cit., p. 194, ll. 29–33.

moderates the pace of her investigations, if the wisdom of God shall have received her and given her rest in the darkness of his hidden places."[32] This is the giving up of meditation, thought of at this time as something that would occur as it were naturally. And so the soul comes to where,

> leaning on her beloved, one flesh, one soul, made one spirit with the One, she is no more separated. And what does the soul do when held intent by these contemplations? What does she say? What does she desire? Without doubt she acts in such a way that she may not be deprived of such a spectacle through her own fault, she prays that she may be removed from her dark prison to these glorious mansions of light, she desires that she may dwell in the house of the Lord all the days of her life, that she may see the delight of the Lord (Psalms 26, 4), and may rest in the courts of God.[33]

It is entirely in keeping with this view of the contemplative life, which we have seen is characteristic of John and Peter, that he says three things concur to bring about this state, good works, protracted prayer, and an ardent desire for God.[34] It is only the first of these that he treats with any clearness, but what he has to say is of great interest in view of John of Fécamp's exhortation to the nun to lead the lives of both Martha and Mary. "The service of the brethren and the daily manual labour, performed in the cloister or the fields as time and necessity demand, form the root of good works. Beyond this, giving alms, visiting the sick, consoling the afflicted, helping widows, receiving the poor and pilgrims, the defence of the oppressed, and such things, are the branches of this tree, not of death but of life, which is called good works."[35] It is a perfectly unequivocal account of the active life, but he takes it for granted that this goes hand-in-hand with the contemplative. In his discursive manner Peter has much to say about the life of union with God, and he uses the phrases

[32] *Ibid.*, p. 211, 11. 17 ff.
[33] *Ibid.*, p. 211, 32 ff.
[34] *Ibid.*, p. 212, 2–8.
[35] *Ibid.*, p. 212, 9–15.

familiar in mystical writers; the soul must be composed and at rest, it must enjoy an *otium quietis*, a peaceful leisure, before it can hear the word of God. Contemplation is a *praelibatio*, a foretaste, of what the soul will experience in heaven.

We see, then, a life centred on the service of God, which includes the service of one's neighbour for God, and this life will lead to a great intimacy with the divine, but it is one which is allowed to grow, as it were, naturally. It was in no way a speculative or intellectual mysticism that Peter of Celle inculcated, but a life of affective prayer nourished on the reading of Scripture, with a background of the liturgy and active good works. Behind it no doubt there lay Augustine's highly intellectual conception of the approach to contemplation. Certainly there were no Augustines in the cloisters of the early Middle Ages, and it may be that their humbler inmates never went beyond some form of affective prayer, but that there were those among them who achieved a high degree of holiness and union with God the writings of John of Fécamp and Peter of Celle do not leave in doubt. The *lectio divina* was a very safe and sound approach to spirituality for people living the retired lives of the monks in the heyday of the monastic system in Western Europe, though it became increasingly less adapted to the needs of the time as the Middle Ages advanced.

THE CISTERCIANS

The Cistercian Order, which was founded at Cîteaux in the year 1098 by St Robert of Molesme, represented a return to primitive Benedictinism. The most widespread of the tenth-century reform movements, that of Cluny, basing itself on the reform of St Benedict of Aniane a hundred years earlier, had greatly developed the liturgical side of monastic life, and had admitted a great number of accretions to the original *cursus* of the Benedictine Office, and as a result of the large amount of time spent on this manual labour had practically ceased to be performed in the Cluniac houses. The Cistercians removed most of the accretions to the Office and returned to the primitive manual labour of the fields, and it was this which constituted the fundamental cleavage between them and the black monks. It is well to remember that Cîteaux was not founded as a protest against what could properly be called abuses, although in an unfortunate controversy which ensued the word came to be bandied about a good deal.

The movement was a purely monastic one, and it was natural that the spirituality of the Cistercians should be fundamentally the same as that of the black monks, but the early Cistercian writers—and all the notable Cistercian writings were produced in the twelfth century, when the Order retained its first fervour—are distinguished by the fact that they were interested in attempting to provide some sort of explanation of the divine action and of the way in which the soul corresponds. But it was not from any purely speculative interest that they broached these questions. They did so always with the view of appreciating better God's love for us, and so of increasing our own for him. That man was originally made in the image of God, that he was placed on terms of friendship and intimacy with him, and that he fell from his privileged position and was restored by the redemption, are facts that are known from revelation. But there are many questions which may be asked. In what sense is man the image of God? What transformation does the image suffer as the result of the Fall? To what degree is it restored, and how is man to cooperate in the restoration? The elucidation of these problems involves a study of the nature of man, of his body and soul, and the relationship between them,[36] as well as raising the further question of the relation

---

[36] This interest is revealed in the number of treatises on the soul produced by the leading Cistercian writers: St Bernard (*De gratia et libero arbitrio*), William of St Thierry (*De natura corporis et animae*), Aelred (*De anima*), Isaac of Stella (*De natura animae et corporis*).

of the soul to God. It was along these lines that the Cistercian writers pursued their inquiries.

With these general ideas in mind we may consider some of the individual writings of the three most important and influential among these authors, St Bernard, St Aelred and William of St Thierry.

ST BERNARD

The figure of St Bernard towers over the whole of the first half of the twelfth century. This Cistercian monk, who entered Cîteaux in 1112, and became abbot of Clairvaux three years later, was the dominant ecclesiastical figure, popes not excepted, in Western Europe at the beginning of the period in which the Church was to exercise her greatest political influence. And yet there is no doubt that in the midst of an intensely active life St Bernard remained a great contemplative. But the anomaly, perhaps, was in playing the rôle he did as a Cistercian monk rather than as a contemplative, for many of the great contemplatives have been men and women of outstanding practical ability and achievement.

In a brilliant analysis of St Bernard's teaching on the spiritual life M. Gilson[37] has maintained that St Bernard consciously set himself to supply the mystical element that was lacking in the *Rule* of St Benedict. St Benedict had stated that his *Rule* was only for beginners, and those who would hasten to the perfection of the monastic life were referred to the teaching of the great Fathers of monasticism (chap. 73). It is true that St Bernard has much to say about the higher reaches of the spiritual life, about contemplation, but it is well to remember that the Benedictines had already in practice achieved contemplation. We have seen that John of Fécamp refers to many kinds. He does nothing to distinguish these various kinds, but that he was aware of what we should

[37] *La Théologie Mystique de Saint Bernard.* Translated by A. H. C. Downes, *The Mystical Theology of St Bernard* (London, 1940).

now call a high degree of infused contemplation seems to be certain from his warning to the nun that she should never think that she had contemplated the essential vision of God.[38] If, then, Bernard aspired after contemplation and achieved it, as he undoubtedly did, this was not something new in medieval monasticism, but what is true of him is that he went much further in analysing the way in which it was to be integrated into the spiritual life, its doctrinal connection with the lower degrees, than the purely Benedictine school had ever done.

St Bernard takes for granted the traditional teaching on the "practical life", the exercise of virtue and the overcoming of sin, and indeed it might be said that his whole edifice is built on humility, to which he devoted a special treatise, the *De humilitate*. By it he meant that true knowledge of ourselves which lays bare the roots of self-love, the legacy of original sin. St Benedict had said that humility would lead to charity, the perfect love which casts out fear, and certainly in effect what St Bernard did was to show how this comes about. He supplied the doctrinal justification, but the thing had been achieved before.

The Love of God

For St Bernard the spiritual life is growth in the love of God, a growth which may lead to ecstasy, and in his work *On the Love of God* he provides an outline of the spiritual life by showing four stages through which the soul must pass. He calls them carnal, mercenary, filial and mystical. By carnal love he means, as M. Gilson has pointed out,[39] a love which is properly directed to God, but which has been degraded to a love of self. It is an inordinate love of self which seeks its good solely in self instead of in God, where our true good lies. So the first step is one of rectification, and it is the work of humility, by which self is subjected to God. A man comes,

[38] See above, page 29.
[39] *The Mystical Theology of St Bernard*, pp. 41 ff.

then, to seek God, but first for the good he can receive from
him, and from there he may be led to love God for his own
sake with a filial love. Between these first three degrees and
the fourth there is a jump. The basic effort to overcome self-
seeking and a false love of self is familiar as the first step in
the religious life. We can understand the transition from a
state in which we are moved primarily by a fear of God's
punishments to one in which the desire to please a loving
God is predominant. But when we come to St Bernard's
treatment of the fourth degree of love it seems not to be
integrated with his other degrees. It does not follow that he
is not justified in putting the experience he goes on to describe
as the culmination of an ascending scale of love for God, but
this last stage is of so different a nature and so entirely the
work of God as not strictly to be comparable with any normal
human experience. And that is indeed the case. What he describes under the fourth degree is in fact contemplation in the
full sense.

> Happy is he, and holy too, to whom it has been given, here
> in this mortal life rarely or even once, for one brief moment
> only, to taste this kind of love! It is no merely human joy to
> lose oneself like this, so to be emptied of oneself as though
> one almost ceased to be at all: it is the bliss of heaven. And yet,
> if some poor mortal do attain to swift and sudden rapture
> such as this, forthwith this present evil world must drag him
> back, the daily ills of life must harass him, the body of this
> death will weigh him down, his fleshly needs cry out for satis-
> faction, the weakness of his fallen nature fails. Most violent
> of all, his brother's needs call on him to return. Alas! he has
> no choice but to come back, back to himself and to his own
> affairs.[40]

The passage is very reminiscent of St Gregory.[41] There is
the same idea of an absorbing experience rarely and with
difficulty attained, a *raptus*, which lasts but a short time, and

[40] I have made use for these passages of the translation made by a
religious of C.S.M.V. in *St Bernard on the Love of God*.
[41] *Hom. Ezech.*, Bk. II, Homil. 2.

then the soul falls back regretfully, and as it were exhausted, to the experiences of everyday life. Very interesting is his remark that it is the need to practise fraternal charity which will most urgently recall the contemplative from contemplation. This is in accord with what John of Fécamp had to say about the desirability of practising both lives, that of Martha as well as that of Mary, and St Bernard elsewhere illustrates his point explicitly from his own experience. He does not grudge time taken from the pursuit of contemplation, he says, for the preparation of his sermons on the *Canticle*, if they are of use to the brethren (Serm. 51, 3). And if in the next sermon he allows himself to complain a little querulously of the intrusions that the community make into his peace, he immediately pulls himself up. "Let them use me as much as they like. I shall be content provided only that they save their souls. They will spare me most by not sparing me at all" (Serm. 52, 7). If St Bernard did go back to Cassian, he did not take over his view of the contemplative life. The text goes on,

> We read in Scripture that God has made all things for himself. His creatures must aim, therefore, at conforming themselves perfectly to their Creator and living according to his will. So we must fix our love on him, bit by bit aligning our own will with his who made all for himself, not wanting either ourselves or anything else to be or to have been, save as it pleases him, making his will alone, and not our pleasure, the object of our desire.

It is a masterly touch; at once we are back from the heights to humility, to the simple conformity of our will to the will of God which, as he will later show more clearly in the sermons on the *Canticle*, constitutes our essential union with God. After this it is only a question of greater realization. St Bernard continues, "O chaste and holy love, affection sweet and holy! O pure and clean intention of the will, the purer in that now at last it is divested of self-will, the lovelier and the sweeter since its perceptions at last are all divine!

To become thus is to be deified." And he goes on to the often used comparisons of the drop of water in the wine and the molten iron in the fire to describe the union of the soul with God. In accordance with this tradition he does not pursue the matter. He uses the word *deify* but he makes no attempt to define it theologically. Essentially his treatment of contemplation here is that which we have met in Gregory, John of Fécamp, and Peter of Celle. It is simply an acknowledgement of the fact.

Sermons on the Canticle

But it is in the sermons on the *Canticle* that he has most to say about the mystical union of the soul with God, and if he is eloquent on the subject, he is so because of his own experience. "I confess, then, though I say it in my foolishness, that the Word has visited me, and even very often", and he goes on to describe the experiences in a manner again very reminiscent of St Gregory, though with greater eloquence. It is important to realize that there was this profound basis for his enthusiasm, even if the manner of its expression was the outcome of natural temperament. Nevertheless, Bernard had his feet on the ground. In more than one place in these sermons dealing explicitly with the contemplative life he takes occasion to remind his hearers of the necessity for practising the fundamental virtues. They must "sow in justice", and he says:

> You have sowed in justice, if by a true knowledge of your-
> selves you have been stirred up to fear God, if you have
> humbled yourselves, if you have shed tears, if you have given
> abundant alms, if you have given yourselves up to works of
> piety, if you have mortified your bodies by fasts and vigils,
> if you have struck your breasts, if you have wearied heaven
> by your cries (*Cant.* XXXVII, 2).

All this must precede the enjoyment of the visitations of the Spirit. And in an interesting and rather touching passage he reveals that he himself was not immune from aridity.

It is not without cause that, for some days past, I feel in myself a languor of soul and stupidity of mind, and an unusual inertia of spirit. I ran well; and behold a stumbling block came in my way; I ran up against it and fell. Pride was found in me, and the Lord being angry turned away from his servant. Hence the sterility of my soul, and the cooling of my devotion. How did my heart thus dry up, thick like curdled milk, like earth without water? I can no longer feel compunction or be moved to tears, so great is the hardness of my heart. The chant of the psalms has no attraction for me; reading is devoid of charm; prayer without consolation. I no longer find my usual meditations. Where is now that inebriation of the spirit, that serenity of mind and peace and joy in the Holy Ghost? Therefore, I am slothful at work, sleepy in vigils, prone to anger, tempted to hatred, self-indulgent in gluttony and the use of the tongue, slothful and dull in preaching. Alas! the Lord visits all the mountains round about me, but he comes not near to me (Serm. 54, 8).[42]

But if the sermons on the *Canticle* were supported by a deep underlying personal experience and were at the same time a reflection of St Bernard's very marked personality, it is also true that fundamentally they conform to the traditional early medieval type of monastic spiritual writing. They are based ultimately on the allegorical interpretation of the scriptural text—at least to the extent that the first two-and-a-half chapters of the *Canticle* provide texts as a starting point for his ideas—and throughout the argument advances by a constant appeal to the authority of Scripture.

But the Cistercians, as has been pointed out, did set out the theological basis of their spirituality in a way that had not previously been done in the West, and it is in a group of these sermons near the end (80–4) that we find St Bernard's clearest exposition of the subject. He introduces the idea of

[42] This and the preceding quotation both appear in the *Meditations on the Life of Christ* attributed to St Bonaventure. I have used the translation of this work made by Sister M. Emmanuel, O.S.B.

the soul being made in the image of God, and following
Augustine he finds an image of the Trinity in the three
powers of the soul, memory, understanding and will. But
it is in man's gift of free will that he particularly finds this
likeness to God, and in sermon 81 on the *Canticle* and in the
treatise *Of Grace* he shows how the essential gift of free will
remains even though the soul has in fact abused its gift in
order to turn from God. The whole process is most clearly
set out in sermon 83. The soul even when it is in sin is still
the image of God, because of its fundamental gift of free will,
but its likeness to God is obscured (it remains *ad imaginem*
but the *similitudo* has been lost). This unlikeness vitiates its
nature, but it does not destroy it (*P.L.*, 183, 1182 B), and the
soul can turn again to the Word to be reformed in itself and
conformed to him. And it is this conformity which weds the
soul to the Word. It is already like him by nature; now it
exhibits its likeness to him through its will, loving even as it
is loved (1182 C). But the Bridegroom of the soul is not
only loving, he is Love itself (1183 A). It is important to see
just what St Bernard means by this union of our love with
the love of God. He goes on to speak of a love in us which
implies a great attraction. This may well be, but the important
thing to realize is that the basis of it is will, not emotion; it
is the conformity of our will to the will of God. This union
of wills is more than a contract; he calls it an embrace, *com-
plexus*, "an embrace in which perfect correspondence of
wills makes of two one spirit" (1182 C). God's will is his
love, and it is a subsistent Personality, the Third Person of the
Trinity. The description that Bernard goes on to give of the
union is psychological. The inequality of the two parties to
the embrace in no way hinders the concurrence of wills, for
love desires nothing but to be loved (1182 D).

> Love that is pure is not mercenary . . . this is the love of the
> Bride, because all that she is is only love. The very being of
> the Bride and her only hope is love (that is her will is wholly

conformed to God). In this the Bride abounds; with this the Bridegroom is content. He seeks for nothing else; she has nothing else. Thence it is that he is Bridegroom and she is Bride. This belongs exclusively to a wedded pair, and to it none other attains, not even a son (1183 D). The Bridegroom's love, or rather the Bridegroom who is love, requires only love in return and faithfulness. Let it then be permitted to the Bride beloved to love in return. How could the Bride not love, she who is the Bride of Love? How could Love not be loved? (1184 A.)

The love of the Bride is as nothing compared to the love of the Bridegroom.

What then, shall the desire of her who is espoused perish and become of none effect, because she is unable to contend with a Giant who runs his course? . . . No. For although, being a creature, she love less, because she is less; nevertheless if she love with her whole self, nothing is wanting where all is given. Wherefore, as I have said, to love thus is to be wedded; because it is not possible to love thus and yet not to be greatly loved, and in the consent of the two parties consists a full and perfect marriage (1184 B). Can anyone doubt that the soul is first loved, by the Word, and more dearly? (1184 C.)[43]

The perfect unity of the spiritual life is manifest. The soul seeks to conform its will—its love—to the Will of God, at first recognized in this and that external circumstance, but the Will of God is the Love of God, is God, and the soul comes increasingly to recognize this, and the more its will is identified with the will of God the more united with God it becomes, until the union is felt in some indescribable but unmistakable way. That was how it was for St Bernard, and he thought it worth his while to relate his feelings in this series of sermons to his monks. How many attained to anything like the heights he reached himself we have no means of knowing, probably very few, but it is perfectly clear that in the

[43] For all these passages I have made use of the translation in Abbot Cuthbert Butler's *Western Mysticism* (1922), pp. 162–5.

Cistercian cloisters of the twelfth century there must have been a widespread desire for union with God.[44]

Devotion to the Humanity of Christ

There is, however, one further important element which St Bernard was very largely responsible for introducing into the spiritual life and that is devotion to the humanity of Christ. We are so used to this that we perhaps assume that it has always existed as we know it now in the Christian Church. It is true that the Church has always prayed *per Christum Dominum nostrum,* but for the first thousand years of her history it was the divinity of Christ that she dwelt on. Nearly always the figure on the cross was Christ in glory, clothed, erect, and with a halo instead of the crown of thorns. We have seen that much of the *Confessio Theologica* of John of Fécamp was in the form of a prayer to Christ, but there is little emphasis on the humanity. John thinks less of the facts of Christ's life than of the essential reality which gives them meaning, the Redemption, though there is tenderness and sensible devotion in the way he speaks of and to our Lord. But in St Bernard's sermons *de Tempore,* delivered to his monks on the great feasts of the Church and in Advent and Lent, we find an intense preoccupation with Christ in his infancy and in the passion, such as is not found in earlier writers. Certainly the thought of Christ's divinity is never far away, and the application of the lesson to ourselves occupies much of the sermons. The actual consideration of the

---

[44] There was a tradition of exegetical commentaries on the *Canticle* from patristic times, in which the text was applied to Christ and the Church or, Christ and the soul. St Bernard in inaugurating a series of monastic commentaries confined it to Christ and the individual soul, and there are at least three Cistercian commentaries in his manner as yet unpublished. The earlier commentaries provided a gloss on the complete text, but the monastic ones were rather treatises *De Amore* in which the text of the *Canticle* is little more than a pretext for a disquisition on the love of God. See J. Leclercq, *Le Commentaire de Gilbert de Stanford sur le Cantique des Cantiques, Studia Anselmiana* (1948), 20, pp. 205–30. See also *Dict. Spirit.,* I, p. 1494.

details of Christ's human life is not so much elaborated as it was later to be, but it is assumed, and the intense emotional eloquence of many passages must have made a profound impression on his hearers, as it undoubtedly influenced later writers. But what is of great importance is to see this devotion to the humanity of Christ in relation to St Bernard's mysticism. It would be true to say that he was as great an exponent of one as of the other, and it follows that they were complementary in his life. For him the one led naturally to the other. Consideration of the humanity was to be spiritualized and to lead to the divinity, but the soul could not long remain in the rarefied atmosphere of pure contemplation, and it had to return from the Word to the Word made Flesh. It was a natural and healthy alternation which was characteristic of the twelfth-century spirituality. At a later period there was to be a tendency to emphasize one at the expense of the other.

ST AELRED

Before going on to say something of William of St Thierry to whom a special interest attaches, a word must be said of St Aelred. Born in 1110, three years before St Bernard entered Cîteaux, he became in Bernard's lifetime the most influential figure among the very strong body of English Cistercians. The list of his works is considerable and as a result of recent scholarship he is beginning to be recognized for the important writer that he was. An intensely human person with a genius for friendship, he must have been less overwhelming than St Bernard. Though not playing any part in current affairs outside strictly monastic circles, he remained interested in recent history—he wrote an account of the battle of the Standard which took place a few miles from Rievaulx soon after he went there—and he was well aware of the problem of integrating the Norman and native elements in the society of his day.[45] However, for our purposes his most important works are the *Mirror of Charity*, written in 1142-3 at the express command of St Bernard, and the book *On Jesus as a Boy of Twelve*,[46] although any complete account of his spirituality would have to take into consideration his treatise *On Spiritual Friendship*, which owes much to Cicero and thus connects him directly with the renewed interest in the classics in the twelfth century, the book he wrote for his sister who was a nun, and his unfinished treatise *On the soul*.

It is in the *Mirror of Charity* that his fullest treatment of the spiritual life is to be found, and as was the case with St Bernard and all the Cistercian writers, his purpose in writing it was primarily practical. The book contains indeed the essence of his teaching as novice-master at Rievaulx, for he was not yet abbot when he wrote it. He sees the spiritual life as man's response to God's love (1-7), but because of his gift of free will man can choose between love of God and love of self. That is the ultimate choice which presents itself (8-15), but if man is to find rest it must be in God and not in creatures, and it is to be achieved by union with Christ through the death of self-will (18-30). That is an attractive way of summarizing the soul's journey to God, stressing as it does first God's love for us, and then the necessity for overcoming self-will, with Christ as the Way. Aelred takes up again, as all these Cistercian writers did, the idea of man being made in the image of God, an image which has been defaced by sin but which it is the business of the spiritual life to restore. He follows Augustine in putting the image of God in the three powers of the soul, memory, understanding and will, powers which in man before the Fall were turned to God and found their object in him. As a result of sin these

---

[45] For a sensitive and illuminating description of Aelred and his background see Sir Maurice Powicke's Introduction to his edition of Walter Daniel's *Life of Aelred of Rievaulx*.
[46] This and the *Letter to his Sister* are now available in English translations in Mowbray's Fleur de Lys series.

powers are dissipated on creatures, but the essential likeness to God remains, although defaced.

In a passage of admirable clarity Aelred shows how our love of God consists essentially in the conformity of our will to God's:

> It is not from passing feelings, which, as every spiritual man knows, are not in the control of our will, that a man must judge his love for God, but rather from the permanent disposition of his will. In effect to love God is to join our will to the will of God so fully that whatever the divine will prescribes the human will consents to, so that it only wills this or that because it knows that God wills it.

That is the essential, unemotional basis of the spiritual life, but Aelred goes on to show to what this union of wills may lead.

> It is the will of God which is his love, and which is nothing else than the Holy Spirit, through whom charity is infused into our hearts. The infusion of this charity is the conjunction of the divine will with the human. And this takes place when the Holy Spirit, who is both the will of God and his love, enters and possesses the human will, and, raising it from lower to higher things, transforms it entirely into his own manner and quality of being, *totam ipsam in sui modum qualitatemque transformat* [the expression conveys perfectly the idea of the union effected by sanctifying grace and no pantheistic meaning need be read into it] so that adhering to him in the unity of an indissoluble association it is made one spirit with him.[47]

That is a simpler, more matter-of-fact, expression of what St Bernard was saying in the eighty-third sermon on the *Canticle*, and it is more theologically satisfying in that it makes explicit the identification of the love of God with the Holy Spirit.

Much more might be said about the spiritual teaching of St Aelred, but it must suffice to mention two points. Aelred brings out, as Bernard for the most part does not, a funda-

[47] *Mirror of Charity*, chap. XVIII; *P.L.*, 195, 566.

mental difficulty of the religious life when an attempt is made
to lead it with any intensity. He wrote the *Mirror of Charity*
while he was still novice-master, and he introduces an anecdote (chap. XVII) which we must believe came from real
life. A novice complains to him that since he has entered the
monastery he feels less religious fervour than he did before.
He suffers the austerities of life at Rievaulx in the first
fervour of the Cistercian movement, but he feels no consolations. Aelred relates the anecdote in the form of a dialogue
between himself and the novice, and he skilfully leads his
interlocutor on to answer his own questions, and to admit
that he is in fact happier in the monastery than he had been
in his life in the world, and he goes on to point out that the
love of God is not to be judged by feelings but by the attitude of the will. The problem was indeed no new one in
the monastic life, it was the old one of *acedia*, which had
been familiar to Cassian, and Aelred himself had already
had much to say on it in the *Mirror* (chaps. XI–XIII). God,
he says, visits the soul three times; the fruit of the first visit
is conversion. The devotion that the novice had experienced
in the world had led him to the religious life. The fruit of
the second is the mortification of self-will, the fruit of the
third is perfect happiness. When the first has done its work
there comes the proving by temptation and labour, which is
itself the work of God (this is what the novice was enduring),
and in due course, in this world or the next, the third will
follow (chap. XIII).

The last point that we may note in Aelred's spiritual
teaching is that same devotion to the humanity of Christ
that we found in St Bernard. The treatise *On Jesus as a Boy
of Twelve* contains a fine meditation on the subject, before
he goes on to allegorical interpretations, but in the book
written for his sister the nun (*Regula Inclusarum*) he develops
a whole system of meditation on the life of Christ, which
makes his work in this respect a forerunner of much that was
to follow.

WILLIAM OF ST THIERRY

In any treatment of Cistercian spirituality in the twelfth century some account must be taken of William of St Thierry. Born in 1085, he became a black monk in the abbey of St Nicasius at Rheims in 1113, and was elected abbot of the neighbouring abbey of St Thierry in 1119. In the previous year, 1118, he had met St Bernard and come under his spell. So much so that it was at his instance that Bernard wrote his apology for the Cistercians, and William as a black monk and an abbot championing the white monks found himself heavily engaged in the controversy between the new Order of the Cistercians and the Benedictines. Finally in 1135 he resigned his abbacy and became a Cistercian himself at Signy in the Ardennes. During the rest of his life, between 1135 and 1148, he wrote much, and it was he who was responsible for raising the opposition to Abelard, though he took no part in the condemnation. It was a visit during these years to the recently founded charterhouse at Mont Dieu that occasioned his most famous work, the *Epistle to the Brethren of Mont Dieu*, the *Golden Epistle* as it came to be called. William is yet another of these medieval writers whose works have only really been brought to light in modern times. For some reason, which is not very well understood, before the end of the twelfth century itself the treatises of William began to be attributed to St Bernard and other writers, and from the end of the Middle Ages until some thirty years ago, apart from a few references by the mystics, little or no attention was paid to them. Modern scholarship, however, has vindicated the claim of William of St Thierry to be considered as a theological and spiritual writer of the first importance. Fr Bouyer, indeed, is tempted to say that as a thinker Bernard in comparison with William does not exist,[48] and M. Gilson, if less outspoken, has paid very high tribute to him as a

[48] *The Cistercian Heritage*, translated by E. A. Livingstone (London, 1958), p. 68.

theologian.[49] Certainly, as was the case with Bernard and
Aelred, William's main purpose in writing was practical.
He was concerned to direct souls in the spiritual life, but his
writings have a coherence and a theological penetration that
is not to be found in any of the other writings of his school.
It will only be possible to say something here of his spirituality as expounded in the *Epistle to the Brethren of Mont
Dieu*. In this work he makes use of the threefold distinction
between beginners, those advancing, and the perfect in the
spiritual life, and it is significant that more than three-
quarters of his book is taken up with the spirituality of
beginners. William had been an abbot, and he knew the
foundations upon which any religious life must rest. He is
writing, it will be remembered, to a charterhouse recently
established which had met with a good deal of external
opposition. He writes to encourage them in their way of life,
but very little of what he says applies only to Carthusians.
For the beginner, in whom what he calls the animal man
predominates, the first necessity is obedience to superiors
(chap. VI, 17).[50] He goes on to speak of mortification, interior
and exterior, examination of conscience, the divine office, the
desirability of making spiritual communions, reading—in
which he inculcates the tradition of spiritual reading we have
met in John of Fécamp and Peter of Celle—food, sleep, etc.
(chap. X). He gives directives about prayer (chap. XIV, 42–6)
in which he makes use of Cassian's fourfold division of prayer
into supplication, intercession, prayer and thanksgiving. The
different techniques of mental prayer had not yet been worked
out, and contemplation was not connected specifically with
prayer as it later came to be, but his description of "pure
prayer" and the prayer of thanksgiving shows that the connection was recognized. It is noteworthy that for the beginner,
he says, "the best and safest things that may be offered for

[49] *The Mystical Theology of St Bernard* (London, 1940), p. 198.
[50] References are to chapters and sections in the English translation
made by Walter Shewring, *The Epistle to the Brethren of Mont Dieu*,
edited by Dom Justin McCann, 1930.

exercising his inward acts are reading and meditating the outward acts of our Redeemer" (chap. XIV, 42), and Meditation X of his *Meditative Prayers* is devoted to this subject. What he has to say on devotion to the humanity of Christ in the *Epistle* is very illuminating, for it shows how for him too this devotion was integrated with contemplation. The humanity was to lead to the divinity. "When he fixeth the gaze of his intention upon him, by considering the human likeness to God, he forsaketh never the truth, and while through faith he severeth not God from man, he learneth at length to apprehend God in man" (chap. XIV, 43), and he goes on to develop the idea.

All this was sound teaching in the monastic tradition, but William's ideals went beyond this. At the very beginning of the *Epistle* he reminds the Carthusians to whom he was writing that their vocation was in fact no new one, but that it went back to the early monasticism of the Egyptian desert (chap. I, 1, 3 and 4). "To others", he says, "it belongeth to serve God, to you to cleave to him; . . . to you to savour of him, to understand him, to apprehend him, to enjoy him" (chap. II, 5). The ideal that he sets before them is a very uncompromising one. Contemplation, and in its more specialized sense, was to be for them not something which might occur in a life dedicated to the service of God, but something the enjoyment of which was to be the conscious end of their lives. Does this go beyond the ideal which St Bernard set before his monks in the sermons on the *Canticle*? It would seem that it does. Bernard had discovered contemplation and is led to expatiate on it, but he never puts its attainment forward as a complete programme. The Cistercian movement after all was a return to primitive Benedictinism. It was this, wisely and skilfully adapted,[51] which its designers sought to establish, and St Benedict did not legislate for the purely contemplative life, which is essentially an eremitical one. Contemplation was known in the Benedictine cloisters, as we

[51] See Knowles, *Monastic Order*, chap. XII.

have seen, but the attainment of it as such had never been the primary end of cenobites.

In William, however, we can see other influences at work. He had made contact with the Greek Fathers who provided the intellectual background to the monks of the desert. This is an interesting fact which has emerged from the researches of Dom Déchanet, who has shown that William's treatise *On the Nature of the Body and the Soul* was largely based on Gregory of Nyssa.[52] This was foundation work for any speculative treatment of spiritual theology, but it does not appear that he had followed Gregory in his treatment of the soul's journey to God in the *Life of Moses*, for example. Still, the fact that he had gone back to the Greek Fathers is of great significance. It represented a development of interest in the theoretic aspect of contemplation, and in the last chapter of the *Epistle* we find him deploying this interest. In calling attention to this purely contemplative ideal, in his appeal to the early pre-Benedictine monachism, and in the use he made of its theological background, William of St Thierry was looking ahead to a movement which was to come after his death.

There is no space to discuss his theology here, but we may just make one observation. He says that a threefold image of God may be found in the soul. From its very nature it has a certain likeness to God which cannot be destroyed; it has a further likeness in so far as virtue is found in it, and above this yet another, which comes about through the unity it has with God from the indwelling of the Holy Spirit (chap. XVI, 62). William does not make clear, as the fourteenth-century writer Walter Hilton was later to do, that this is really sanctifying grace and that it is not different, save in degree, from the grace that any soul receives at baptism.

It was to be expected that the Cistercian contribution

[52] *Aux Sources de la Spiritualité de Guillaume de Saint-Thierry* by J.-M. Déchanet, O.S.B.

to spirituality in the first fervour of the order would be outstanding, and there is no doubt that the fullest expression of the type which was characteristic of the Middle Ages up to the end of the thirteenth century is to be found in their writings.[53]

THE CARTHUSIANS

The institution of the Carthusian order by St Bruno in 1098 established on a firmer and wider basis the quasi-eremitical life that had been begun in Italy earlier in the century.[54] But the Carthusians in fact introduced no new element. Perhaps their best-known contribution to the spiritual writings of this period was the piece variously called *Scala Paradisi, Scala Claustralium,* or the *Tractatus de quattuor gradibus spiritalibus,* in a Middle English version *A Ladder of Four Rungs.*[55] The four rungs are reading, meditation, prayer, and contemplation. In distinguishing prayer from contemplation it introduces a distinction unusual at

[53] It is perhaps worth mentioning that a number of anonymous tracts, apparently contemporaneous with the Cistercian movement, give an admirable exposition of this spirituality at a rather lower level than that at which we have been considering it. They consist largely of excerpts from known authors, but they differ from the type of *florilegium* that John of Fécamp produced in that they are not so much designed to lead directly to prayer, as to give a conspectus of the whole spiritual life as seen in this affective approach. They all follow the same simple and fundamental plan in so far as they are all built upon the consideration of two subjects, God and the human soul. Some of the treatises, e.g. the *Liber Soliloquiorum* (P.L., 40, 863), *De contritione cordis* (P.L., 40, 943) and *De humana conditione* (P.L., 184, 485) are more concerned with the human aspect of their subject, with sin and the weakness of human nature, and they tend to take a sombre view, reflecting, it may be supposed, the influence of Augustine in his anti-Pelagian writings. Others, e.g. the *De interiori domo* (P.L., 184, 507), the *Manuale* (P.L., 40, 951), and the *De anima* (P.L., 177, 171) lay more stress on aspiration after union with God. The word *contemplation* is hardly mentioned, but what obviously amounts to no less than some degree of it is the object of ardent desire.

[54] See above, page 32.

[55] The Latin text is printed twice in Migne, *P.L.,* 40, 997–1004, and *P.L.,* 184, 475–84. The Middle English version, which is free and rather expanded, has been printed in a modernized form by Dom Justin McCann (Stanbrook, 1953). There is also a modern English version of the Latin by Fr Bruno Scott James, *The Scale of the Cloister.*

this time, but the stages are obviously essentially the ones we have seen. A less well-known work, the *Fourfold Exercise of the Cell*,[56] is interesting in that it analyses the process of meditation, and the analysis demonstrates very well how meditation could turn into contemplation. Later the Order was to be closely connected with the mystical movement of the later Middle Ages in England. There is much evidence from the manuscripts of their interest in this literature, but they did not actually contribute to it.

THE GERMAN NUNS: SS. HILDEGARDE, ELIZABETH, GERTRUDE AND MECHTILDE

Before passing on to a brief survey of spirituality outside the strictly monastic orders, a word may be said of a rather curious development which occurred in the Benedictine Order. Four nuns in German convents, Saints Hildegarde and Elizabeth of Schonau in the twelfth century, and Saints Gertrude and Mechtilde in the thirteenth, were all the recipients of extraordinary mystical graces. They were ecstatics and visionaries, and to that extent in marked contrast to the contemplatives of the monastic tradition, for of these from the time of St Gregory onwards it seems to be true, as Abbot Cuthbert Butler pointed out, that they exhibited very little of what he called the psycho-physical concomitants of mysticism. But if these German nuns stood apart from the tradition in this respect, they showed no real affinities with the mystical school that was to appear in the fourteenth century.[57] There is no evidence of a theory of contemplation, or of any sort of a cult of it, of a deliberate turning away from the use of the imagination in order the better to attain

[56] The *Liber de quadripartito exercitio cellae* is printed in Migne, *P.L.*, 153, 799–884. It was, once again, Dom Wilmart who was responsible for assigning its authorship definitely to the Scot, Adam of Dryburgh, who became a Carthusian at Witham in Somerset about 1187. See *Auteurs Spirituels*, p. 248.

[57] Perhaps this influence was present in the contemporary of the last two, Mechtilde of Magdeburg. The Dominican influence in German convents was beginning to make itself felt. See chapter III below.

it. All their experiences seem to have been unlooked for, and even, as regards their more ecstatic manifestations, unwanted, and their visions all seem to have been imaginary ones inspired most frequently by the liturgy. All of the four who have attained celebrity—but there were others: it was a strong tendency in some convents—became recognized as saints, though they were not all formally canonized, and their lives were made impressive by the practice of great virtue, the only sure hallmark of genuine mystical experience. It is evident that they belonged essentially to the monastic tradition, as they could hardly help doing, but why in their case this should have produced so striking a demonstration it is perhaps not possible to say. We can only note for what it is worth that they were all women and all Germans.

Much time has been spent in trying to give some idea of the spiritual ideals current in the early Middle Ages, and of the means taken to achieve them, because by the time the Cistercians had made their contribution it could be said that all the ingredients were there of a spirituality which remained substantially the same until the movement of mystical theology properly so-called spread over North-west Europe in the fourteenth century. The spirituality of the early Middle Ages had been necessarily monastic, but with the appearance of other forms of the religious life, the canons regular and the friars, it came to be developed in slightly different ways and with varying emphases. It must suffice here to say only a very few words about the more important of these developments.

THE VICTORINES

A distinction should perhaps be made at this point between practical and speculative spirituality. From a practical point of view it seems that there was little change. Cistercian spirituality continued to provide the norm, but already in the twelfth century in the writings of the canons regular of St Victor outside Paris the new intellectual movement of

scholasticism made some impact on spirituality in the speculative field, though even here the development was fundamentally that of the Augustinian tradition. They applied with
great thoroughness Augustine's symbolist conception of the
universe. All material things symbolized spiritual truths, but
as the result of original sin man had stopped at the material,
made it an end in itself, and was unable to reach the realities
it symbolized. It was the work of the Redemption to enable
man by the contemplation of the visible to rise once more
to the contemplation of the invisible, first to the nature of the
soul and of angels, and then by the revelation of God to the
divinity itself.[58] In their thorough application of symbolism to
the spiritual life the Victorines were only pushing to their
logical conclusion ideas that had come into Christianity with
the Greek Fathers, and through the allegorical interpretation
of Scripture had never ceased to exercise an influence. In so
far as they sought the knowledge of God in himself through
an intuitive process and not knowledge about him through a
process of reasoning, the Victorines were entirely in the
monastic tradition, which it will be remembered would itself
seem to have derived through Augustine from the Greek
conception of *theologia*. Their symbolist view of the universe
lent itself to an intuitive rather than a dialectical method of
approaching God and led naturally to a greater emphasis on
contemplation, and the contemplation even here on earth of
the Godhead became for them the specific goal to be aimed
at in the spiritual life. They were the first medieval writers
to become really interested in the speculative aspect of
mysticism, but their influence though great in that sphere did
not extend beyond it.

THE THIRTEENTH CENTURY:
DOMINICANS AND FRANCISCANS

With the thirteenth century we find the change that was
coming over society in North-west Europe beginning to be

[58] *Quodlib.*, VII, art. XIV, ad 4.

reflected in the spirituality. It was not so much that new practices were introduced or a new approach adopted. Generally speaking they were not, but conditions had changed greatly since the beginning of our period. Europe was growing up. The old Roman civilization had perished under the impact of successive barbarian invasions, and the society which survived to lick its wounds in the tenth century was reduced to a cultural level not much higher than that of its latest enemies, the Norsemen. But once a condition of stability had been reached the natural process asserted itself by which—granted the presence of some stimulus, in this case Christianity—a people develops with a development analogous to that of an individual. Even the old classical culture, on which a very tenuous hold had been maintained, began to revive, and in due course the schools emerged from the monasteries to the clergy houses of the cathedral cities, and eventually universities grew up. In the nature of things, it would seem, scholasticism, the application of reason to the data of revelation, came into being. It was helped, of course, by the increasing rediscovery of the ancient culture, and also by external circumstances. For the laity were becoming more educated and articulate. In early feudal days the laity had consisted of two classes, on the one hand the serfs, and on the other the feudal lords and their retainers. Neither group was literate or interested in the things of the mind. By the thirteenth century, in southern Europe at any rate, sections of the laity were becoming articulate to the extent of expressing criticism of existing social conditions and the lives of the clergy, and sufficiently intellectual to foster a neo-Manichaean movement of some magnitude.[59] It was a situation which the monasteries, with their tradition of an enclosed and isolated life devoted to the individual pursuit of holiness, were in no way fitted to deal with, although the Cistercians made an effort. The sign of life in a

[59] The first of these manifestations was represented by the Waldenses, the second by the Albigenses.

body is that it exerts itself against anything which threatens its existence, and the Church was bound to show such a sign, and under the providence of God the form it took was the emergence of the new Orders of friars. The Dominican Order was consciously and explicitly designed to meet the new situation, and from the start it equipped itself to defend and propagate the faith. The instrument of scholasticism was ready to its hand, and the need constituted the external stimulus which was required for its full development. The origins of the Franciscan Order were more complex, but even in its most primitive state the apostolic motive was not lacking. It is easy to see that these new forms of the religious life would have their effect on spirituality. This was not in fact so great as might have been expected, and on the whole it retained its traditional character. The scholastic theologians for the most part did not write treatises on the spiritual life as such—St Bonaventure was the great exception—but their speculations necessarily had bearing on the theory. The works of pseudo-Denis as interpreted by Thomas Gallus began to exercise influence, as they had already done on the Victorines, and there were necessarily many currents and cross-currents, but in general the work of this great period of intellectual activity in so far as it affected spirituality was to clarify the Augustinian conception of an ever-increasing intellectual illumination culminating in contemplation.

On the practical plane new conditions were bound to modify methods. In the new Orders there was simply no time for the old meditative reading, the monastic *lectio divina*; the exigencies of study and the "quest" did not leave room for it. Nor did the new theology help the situation. With the application of dialectic to theology this became a speculative science, and while it was no doubt prepared to defend the speculative knowledge of God as an end in itself, it had also the motive of the defence and exposition of the faith. In either case the new theology was concerned with knowledge *about* God, and at once we see the difference between it and the older monastic type. For the monastic writers, as for the Victorines, the object of theology was the knowledge of God in himself. They thought of it as the process of actually attaining him in so far as he can be attained in this life. The old theology was spirituality, the new in practice was, or could be, divorced from it; the one no longer flowed naturally and directly from the other.

St Dominic was aware of the danger of too great absorption in study for his Preachers, and just because it was their purpose to go out into the world to preach, he provided them with a background of the traditional life of the cloister, which was to serve at once as a safeguard and a source of spiritual strength. If the old type of meditative reading was necessarily absent, there was the recitation of the divine Office in choir and the traditional ascetic practices in a rather severe form. His greatest follower, St Thomas, had no occasion to deal explicitly with the spiritual life, though his theology was later to exercise an important influence, but for him the highest life was that which combined, as the life of his Order was designed to do, contemplation with preaching. *Contemplata aliis tradere*, to hand on the fruits of contemplation, at least in a wide sense, summed up the ideal of the Friars Preachers.

The Franciscan way of life harmonized very easily with the old spirituality, reproducing all its features but to some extent varying the emphasis. The original idea of St Francis had been simply the imitation of the life of Christ in all its simplicity and poverty. That was the life that he himself led, and it remained the ideal of a large number of his followers. It is easy to see how such an attitude took up naturally that devotion to the humanity of Christ which the Cistercians had already introduced into their spirituality. It was not just a question of meditating on the human life of Christ, but of actually living a life which was to be as close an imitation of it as possible. The difficulty, of course, was that such a life could not be organized on a large scale, and with the accession of large numbers organization became imperative. This is not the place to discuss the difficulties that ensued. To a large extent the original ideal was modified, as it was, for example, in the matter of preaching. A simple form of this had been intended to form part of the life from the start, but it is not an activity that can be carried on by a large number of untrained men without producing undesirable results, of which the Church at this very time had just had experience,[60] and the necessity of training preachers made it inevitable that the new Order should be caught up in the scholastic movement. The Franciscans indeed came to supply many of its most prominent figures, and it was one of these, St Bonaventure, who in seventeen years as Minister General performed the difficult task of getting the Order on to an even keel, and it is of interest to note the interpretation of the ideals of St Francis which he put forward.[61] There were to be three elements in the life; following in the footsteps of Christ in the life of the evangelical counsels, especially poverty, labouring for the salvation of souls by preaching and hearing confessions, and contemplation. The inspiration of St Francis on Monte Alverno remained, and the contemplative element was never lacking in the Order, but it is clear that for the Franciscans as for the Dominicans the ideal was not the purely contemplative life; it was essentially a life into which the rôles of both Martha and Mary should enter. Just

[60] The Church had much difficulty with the Waldenses on this precise point.

[61] *Determinationes Quaestionum circa Regulam FF. Minorum*, Pt. I, Q.1. Translated by Fr D. Devas, O.F.M., in *St Bonaventure and the Religious Life*. See pp. 10–11.

The limited scope of this little volume does not permit any extended treatment of St Bonaventure. He was learned, a doctor of the University of Paris, a commentator on the *Sentences* of Peter Lombard in the scholastic manner, and touched by all the formative influences in the theology of his time, but fundamentally in him speculative theology was wedded to the older conception, the Augustinian idea of theology as ultimately the contemplation of the great mysteries of God under divine illumination. In his *Itinerarium mentis in Deum* he is really analysing and schematizing in the scholastic manner the traditional monastic approach to contemplation through theology.

how much the Franciscan spirituality followed the traditional monastic lines can be seen from the *Meditations on the Life of Christ* long attributed to St Bonaventure.[62] They were written in the first quarter of the fourteenth century by an unnamed friar of Tuscany, who has still not been identified, and because they incorporated well-known meditations on the Passion by St Bonaventure the whole collection came to pass under his name. The interesting thing about this work is the great number of passages quoted from St Bernard. In particular a whole treatise on the active and contemplative lives (chaps. 45–58) is inserted, which consists largely of quotations from the sermons of St Bernard. The work was immensely popular, and so as late as the fourteenth century the Franciscans were still drawing freely on the monastic sources of the twelfth century for their spirituality.

But the explicit relation of the Franciscan life to the life of Christ, which was never lost sight of among all the developments of the Order, had undoubtedly a profound effect on the tone of medieval spirituality in general from the thirteenth century onwards. As has been pointed out, it was only the development of an existing tendency, but we find it now deployed in accordance with the needs of the age for the benefit of the laity. A tender devotion to the humanity of Christ and, as a natural corollary, to his Mother, appears as the predominant characteristic both of the vernacular religious verse, which was beginning to be abundant, and of religious art. References to our Lady in John of Fécamp are incidental, though recourse to her intercession is taken for granted. Among the English Benedictines of the eleventh century there

[62] There is an English translation by Sister M. Emmanuel, O.S.B. (London, 1934). These meditations were largely superseded at the end of the fourteenth century by the *Life* of Christ written by Ludolph of Saxony (Ludolph the Carthusian, 1300–70). This was a more complete *Life*, but of course quite different from what we expect such a work to be now. The author did not hesitate to draw on apocryphal sources or on his imagination, and his only end was to make his readers love and imitate Christ. Both these works will have formed a suitable supplement to the anonymous treatises referred to earlier in this chapter (p. 61, n. 53).

was strong support for the doctrine of the Immaculate Conception, and Eadmer, the biographer of St Anselm, wrote a
notable treatise on the subject, but St Bernard (followed in
this by Peter of Celle) was not an advocate of the doctrine,
and his influence may have been instrumental in pushing it
into the background.[63] He had nevertheless intense devotion to
our Lady and some of his most eloquent sermons are devoted
to her. From the twelfth century devotion to the humanity
of Christ and devotion to Mary go hand-in-hand.[64]

[63] See Knowles, *Monastic Order*, pp. 510–14.
[64] For the reflection of this in vernacular verse see Carleton Brown's
Religious Lyrics of the Thirteenth Century and *Religious Lyrics of the
Fourteenth Century, passim.*

CHAPTER III

THE MYSTICAL MOVEMENT OF THE FOURTEENTH CENTURY

From about the beginning of the fourteenth century a new movement in spirituality begins to be discernible in the Rhineland, the Low Countries and England. The older tradition, of course, was not lost sight of, and necessarily they had much in common. Nevertheless, a new trend in spirituality is very clearly recognizable. Indeed trend is not the right word, because it was not something which grew out of the existing method, but something which was introduced from without. Essentially, it was a new attitude to contemplation and an attempt to analyse it which was quite foreign to the tradition we have been considering. From the early Middle Ages, as we have seen, the term contemplation was used to cover almost any single-minded and intense effort to seek God, but the word was also used to describe the higher, what might be called the experimental, union of the soul with God. As the Middle Ages advanced a more speculative interest was taken in this higher union, which is con-templation proper, and the Victorines and St Bonaventure moved towards a definition of it in the Augustinian tradition.

But the spirituality which was developed in the lands of the eastern Mediterranean between the third and the sixth century contained, as we have seen, two elements. There was on the one hand the idea that to the meditative and prayerful consideration of the Christian mysteries there would come the illumination of the Holy Spirit, and the process might culminate in a true experience of contemplation. This was the *theologia* of the Greeks. On the other hand there was the tradition of the contemplative life, strongly coloured by Neo-Platonic philosophy, the effort to find rest in the unity of God, and the conception of contemplation that had been worked out in connection with this. It has been our thesis that in the West the first of these ideas predominated throughout the early Middle Ages. Broadly speaking it would be true to say that what happened now was that the second element, all along predominant in the East, and which had already begun to influence the scholastic thinkers, came to exercise a predominant influence on spirituality in Northwest Europe.

That the new approach to spirituality stemmed ultimately from the lands of the eastern Mediterranean is not in doubt. It has long been recognized that the greatest single influence on the new school of writers was that of pseudo-Denis, and a word must be said about him. He was probably a Syrian monk who lived about the year 500, who chose to identify himself as an author with Denis the Areopagite mentioned in Acts 17. 34, and throughout the Middle Ages his works had a quasi-apostolic authority as a result of this identification. The work of Denis represented a development of the Neo-Platonic, contemplative tradition in Christianity. In the Augustinian tradition, the two elements, the contemplative and the theological as we may call them, were balanced in the sense that while contemplation of God was the ultimate goal, the act of contemplation itself, however transcendent and excluding everything of sense and imagination, was yet intellectual in so far as it was the climax of an ever increasing illumination. It was the metaphor of light which was used to describe it. Truly the light, the infusion of knowledge, might become such that the ordinary power of the intellect could not apprehend it, and it was only received by a special enablement of God. Consequently, when the soul returned to its normal level of action, it was unable to find words adequate to express what it had experienced. But it was led up to this experience by an increasing illumination. Denis and Gregory of Nyssa before him described the whole process by the metaphor of darkness. The knowledge of God acquired in contemplation was a transcending or going beyond the intellect, which indeed it had been in effect for the others. Since this direct knowledge of God was not in the ordinary sense intellectual, it followed that the use of the intellect could only get in its way by, as it were, substituting a lower form of knowledge, and hence came the necessity for giving up the use of the intellect in order to attain to contemplation of God. This was the "abandonment" demanded by all writers of this school.

The writings of Denis were translated into Latin by Scotus Erigena in Carolingian times, but the breathing space in the Dark Ages afforded by the strong rule of Charles the Great was so short that they quickly became lost to sight. The Victorines knew them in the twelfth century and made some use of them, but it was only after Thomas Gallus had translated and commented on the works of Denis in the first half of the thirteenth century that they began to exercise a strong influence in the West. It should be noted that Dionysian contemplation as expounded by Gallus was less exclusively intellectual and laid more emphasis on love than the original. The approach to spirituality which we have been studying was through a meditative consideration of the Christian mysteries. Now the scheme was to leave the meditation of mysteries and to concentrate the mind on the simplest idea of God. It was the cult of contemplation. Not only the exterior world had to be abandoned but the interior as well, not only all created things but even the thought of them, and this was extended to the humanity of Christ. By its best representatives this spirituality was surrounded by qualifications and safeguards and was fully integrated with the Christian life, but that it had its dangers its greatest exponents were well aware.

Throughout the Middle Ages there was a gradual development and diffusion of learning, and we have already had occasion to notice[1] how the Eastern theologians, particularly Origen and Gregory of Nyssa, were becoming known and beginning to exert an influence on spirituality in the twelfth century. It was in the natural course of things that the writings of pseudo-Denis should in their turn attract attention. Cognizance was bound to be taken of them as part of the general widening of the intellectual landscape that was taking place in the thirteenth century, and we have seen that it was. That they should have come to exercise the influence they did in the spirituality of the following century was perhaps not so inevitable. A reason may be found, as Denifle suggested, in the twofold fact that there was a great increase in the number of convents for women, and particularly of the Dominican Order, in the Germanic lands during the thirteenth century, and that the Dominican friars were made responsible for the supervision of these nunneries.[2] The task was confided to the masters and lectors in theology, with the result that a number of highly trained theologians became responsible for the spiritual care of a large number of fervent and educated women. The circumstances offered an ideal opportunity for applying this highly specialized spirituality which had come to the notice of the learned world. But there were other and wider influences at work. The whole temper of the times seems to have been conducive to the mystical approach to religion. What the conditions were which favoured such a temper cannot be discussed here, but the invasion of scholastic philosophy by Nominalism, political

[1] Chap. II, p. 60.
[2] See Clark, *The Great German Mystics*, p. 4. The reasons for this development of religious life among women are outside the scope of this book. The absence of many upper-class men at the Crusades was almost certainly a contributing factor.

and ecclesiastical troubles, interdict and schism, even the natural calamities of plague and famine and earthquake, may all have contributed. In times of stress, when their world threatens to fall about them, and what have been accepted values are no longer accepted, men will tend to turn to God, and the appeal especially of a personal, immediate communion with him will be very strong. Our own day has not been lacking in manifestations of this tendency. In the fourteenth century the whole of the Rhine valley was seething with religious enthusiasts, Beguines and Beghards, and Brethren of the Free Spirit, some of them controlled and respectable, some of them not.[3] The directors of the nuns were of course well aware of the religious *milieu*, for they preached many sermons in crowded churches, but, unless Eckhart did so through inadvertence, they did nothing to foster the excesses.

THE GERMAN SCHOOL

The known writers who gave expression to this very distinctive spirituality are only four in number, though the large number of anonymous manuscripts which in the past have been attributed to these authors witnesses to the fact that their influence was widespread. Three of them were Germans and Dominicans, Eckhart (*c.* 1260–*c.* 1327), Tauler (*c.* 1300–*c.* 1350), and Suso (*c.* 1300–66). The fourth, Ruysbroeck (1293–1381), was a Fleming who was first a secular priest in Brussels and later a canon regular of St Augustine at Groenendael.

The teaching of all these writers was fundamentally the same. In the strict sense they form a school, and perhaps it would be well to make clear at once that for all of them the cultivation of contemplation was something which presupposed the practice of a virtuous life. They themselves were trained in the traditional "practical" life, and they never ceased to inculcate the necessity for it. But, taking this for

[3] For a short account of this background see Clark, *ibid.*, pp. 1 and 2.

granted, the question with which they particularly concerned themselves was that of the soul's union with God. It is
well to remember that for them, as for their sources, there
was a scriptural background. The texts are familiar enough
and it will suffice to quote a few samples: "See how God
has shown his love towards us: that we should be counted as
his sons, should be his sons" (1 John 3. 1). "Through him
God has bestowed on us high and treasured promises; you
are to share the divine nature, with the world's corruption,
the world's passions, left behind" (2 Peter 1. 4). And there are
of course the well-known Pauline texts. "All those who from
the first were known to him, he has destined from the first
to be moulded into the image of his Son, who is thus to
become the oldest-born among many brethren" (Rom. 8. 29).
"Through faith in Jesus Christ you are all now God's sons.
All you who have been baptized in Christ's name have put
on the person of Christ" (Gal. 3. 26–7), and, "Yet I am alive;
or rather not I; it is Christ that lives in me" (Gal. 2. 20). It
was in contemplation that they saw this union at its fullest,
and instead of contenting themselves with a practical and
experimental approach to it, as the earlier medieval writers
had done, they carried the analysis of the process very far.
They were theologians, and though for them contemplation
was achieved by a non-intellectual process, the theory in
itself of course was highly intellectual. It was indeed intellectual in the strict sense, for it was based on certain
theological principles, and it fearlessly carried these to
their conclusions, whatever obscurities the process might
involve.

In briefest outline the theory might be put thus. They described the union between God and the soul as the birth of
the Word in the "ground" or "spark" of the soul, and in
order that this might take place the soul had to renounce
all created things, to practise complete detachment or abandonment. The spark, or ground, of the soul was an idea about
which these writers, and particularly Eckhart, speculated

deeply. What they meant by saying that the union took place in the ground of the soul was that it was not in the intellect, as that power was understood by the scholastics; it was at an altogether deeper level, in what might be called the essence of the soul, and it was in fact sometimes spoken of as essential union. The intellect knows through images, but in its ground the soul is free from images, and God can unite himself to it freely without form or similitude. It was the union of the simple essence of the soul with the essential Being of God, and when they spoke of the birth of the Word in the ground of the soul, they meant the penetration of God into it, his communication with the essence of the soul. They saw the ground of the soul as the image or reflection of God —man was made in the image of God—and the birth of the Word in the soul was a sort of actualization of this image; this was what they meant by saying that the creature returned to its dwelling-place in the Word, where its Idea existed eternally. All this was necessarily mysterious, and Eckhart got into trouble from the fact that he, as it were, did violence to both thought and language in trying to express it. But the point to seize is that the union took place beyond the reaches of intellect. According to the Dionysian teaching which they followed, the intellect could not know God. He so far transcends man that human categories simply do not apply to him. Thus Suso says, "If anyone calls him 'Godhead' or 'Being', or whatever name one gives him, they are not appropriate to him in the sense in which these names are applied to creatures".[4] And a little later he says we can penetrate more deeply into God "when we are able to understand without the light of forms or images of any kind, the things which indeed no intelligence that operates by means of forms or images can attain".[5] Hence it was that they

[4] *Little Book of Truth*, chap. 5. Translated by J. M. Clark, *Little Book of Eternal Wisdom and Little Book of Truth*, p. 191.
[5] *Ibid.*, p. 192.

demanded as the necessary immediate preparation for this union not only the abandonment of all creatures, but of all thought of them. All images, even of the humanity of Christ, must be rejected. The author of the English treatise *The Cloud of Unknowing* was to give perhaps the clearest practical exposition of this.

ECKHART

Eckhart became a controversial figure in his own day, and to some extent has remained so ever since. A doctor of the University of Paris and provincial of Saxony, he was a man of considerable standing in the Dominican Order and in the Church in Germany, but at the end of his life he was condemned for teaching heresy by the court of the archbishop of Cologne. He appealed to the pope, but died before a decision had been given, though after his death certain propositions taken from his works were censured. The difficulty was caused by the fact that Eckhart was intensely interested in the speculative question of the nature of the soul's union with God, and in his efforts to express the closeness of that union he used, as many mystics have done, language which at its face value appeared to be pantheistic. Eckhart speaks on occasion as though the soul were completely identified with the divinity, and propositions could be, and were, taken from his works, which as they stand in isolation are exaggerated and incorrect, but there is little doubt in view of his writings as a whole that his meaning was orthodox. Today it is easy for us to be dispassionate about the teaching of a fourteenth-century mystic, but in his own day Eckhart was a popular preacher in German whose sermons became widely diffused, and at the root of the many undisciplined and errant lives which were masquerading under the cloak of mysticism at the time was always to be found a pantheistic interpretation of the union of the soul with God. And it always led to the same aberration, the idea that the soul so united was free from the possibility of sin. What the body did was of no consequence, and the commandments of God could be ignored. It would be fantastic to identify such teaching with the writings of Eckhart, but with such ideas going about one can understand that contemporary authority would be nervous, and the theologians were justified in condemning what he actually said as distinct from what in fact he may have meant. The difficulty was aggravated by the fact that to an intensely speculative mind Eckhart added an ineradicable tendency to bold and paradoxical expressions.

There is, or has been, a good deal of difficulty in establishing the text of Eckhart's writings and it may be well to say a word on the subject. He wrote in Latin and German, but also preached much in German, and it is by his German sermons that he is still best known. But our texts of his German sermons depend only on notes taken by his hearers, so clearly they are not an altogether reliable witness to his thought. Then, as a result of his condemnation, his works suffered an almost total eclipse for centuries. Some of the Latin works indeed seem to have disappeared completely, though the German sermons, with an uncertain textual history to start with, continued to be copied, and led a sort of underground existence, suffering still further by later unscholarly editing. It was only in the early nineteenth century, under the influence of a rather wild religious revivalism in Germany, that interest began to be taken in his writings again, and this led to an uncritical enthusiasm which is reflected in Pfeiffer's edition of 1857, until recently the standard German edition of his works. Pfeiffer attributed some hundred and ten sermons and eighteen tracts to him. When the uncertainty of many of these attributions came to be realized, there was a reaction, and at the beginning of this century scholars were hardly willing to allow the genuineness of any of his works. Since then a completely new start has been made, and a group of German scholars is in the process of bringing out a definitive edition of Eckhart.[6] The work is not yet complete, but as a result of the researches which have been made thirty sermons and four tractates in German[7] are definitely attributed to him. In Latin his large work, the *Opus Tripartitum*, which he himself describes, is only known in a few commentaries on passages from Scripture. There are about fifty Latin sermons, some of which are only in note form.

It was his fellow Dominican, Denifle, who pointed out at the end of last century the necessity of taking his Latin works into consideration before any complete judgement can be made on him, and that he had a claim to be considered a theologian of some standing. He remains a difficult writer, and in spite of the large amount that has been written on him in recent years no definite assessment has yet been made of his work, but of his leading place in the stream of spirituality which arose in Western Europe in the fourteenth century there can be no doubt. He was interested primarily in the ultimate goal of the spiritual life as he saw it, the achievement of this essential union with the Godhead, and the ideas of the spark or ground of the soul, the birth of the Word in it, and of abandonment, are the constant themes of his writings.

TAULER

Tauler, also a Dominican, was his acknowledged disciple, but he wrote after Eckhart's condemnation and he was careful to guard himself against the errors for which his master had been condemned. He did not suffer the eclipse which Eckhart suffered, but much legend accumulated about his name, and many works were attributed to him which

[6] *Meister Eckhart, Die deutschen und lateinischen Werke* (Stuttgart, 1936), etc. The most convenient introduction in English is *Meister Eckhart, Selected Treatises or Sermons translated from Latin and German with an Introduction and Notes* by James M. Clark and John V. Skinner (London, 1958). See select bibliography there.
[7] The tractates are: *Talks of Instruction, Book of Consolation, The Nobleman, On Detachment.*

modern scholarship has pronounced spurious. All his writings, it is agreed now, were in German, and consist of the sermons and one letter.[8] Tauler's sermons contain much very valuable spiritual teaching. He lays sure foundations. The beginning of all spiritual life is to strive earnestly to rid oneself of sins, first gross ones and then more subtle ones. The greater part of his sermons, in fact, consist in practical teaching, concerned primarily with the inner asceticism of the spirit, and they give an admirable exposition of it. His sermons are essentially the spoken word, full of homely illustrations and comparisons. He must have been much more in touch with his audience, one would guess, than Eckhart was, though one can glimpse sometimes the fascination that Eckhart must have exercised on an audience perhaps only imperfectly comprehending what he said. For the most part Tauler is easy to understand, but almost always he introduces the theme of detachment, of giving up everything for God, in the sense of renouncing all *desire* and committing ourselves entirely to the divine will in order to be able to receive the visit of God and hear his voice in the soul. The degree of detachment at which he aimed, as with all these writers, involved the giving up of thought, of images—in effect this meant in prayer and spiritual exercises, not, obviously, in the conduct of the ordinary business of life, though this was to be reduced to a minimum. "To hear this interior voice, the best thing we can do is to listen in repose and silence. When God speaks all must be quiet. If God is to act in us, we must allow him to act and give him place, for he cannot act if we are exerting ourselves in our own way" (Vetter, *Serm.* 43). That is his constant advice, but only now and again will he launch

[8] The standard edition is that of Vetter (1910), but it is not entirely satisfactory. Interest in him has waned as that in Eckhart has grown, and little has been done. In English there is virtually nothing on him except Clark, *The Great German Mystics*, S. Winkworth, *The History and Life of the Rev. Dr. John Tauler of Strasbourg* (London, 1857), and a small but excellent modern selection, *Signposts to perfection, a selection from the sermons of J. Tauler*, selected, edited and translated by E. Strakosch (London, 1958).

forth into a description of what may ensue from such a withdrawal. Thus in his sermon for Christmas (Vetter, *Serm.* 1) he
speaks of the threefold birth of the Word; by the eternal
generation of the Son in the divine Essence, by the birth of
Jesus in the world, and by the birth of God in the soul. Before
the latter can take place, there must be this return of the soul
to itself, an interior concentration of all its powers, the lowest
as well as the highest. It is the results of the Fall which make
this process difficult, but in so far as he achieves it, a man will,
as it were, step above himself, leaving mundane activity and,
most important, the implication of his own will and desire
in it, far below. All self-interest and selfish aims must be
abandoned in order that he may exist only for God and
obey him in all things, both great and small. In this way the
birth of the Word (God's action) in the soul will be unhindered, and if the dwelling-place is prepared, it must needs
be that God will fill it.

In the sermon for the Monday before Palm Sunday (Vetter,
Serm. 11) he speaks of the storms and agitations that may arise
in the lower powers of the soul, but God dwells in the higher
powers—according to the full Eckhartian doctrine even above
these—and this dwelling-place of God he describes as a wild
desert of which no man can speak, the hidden darkness of
the modeless good (*des weiselosen Gutes*). The higher powers
of the soul are lost in the simple, modeless unity where all
multiplicity is lost and unity unifies all multiplicity.[9] Yet after
this the soul will have a great understanding of all the articles
of the faith, because none understand true distinction better
than those who attain to unity—there is ineffable darkness yet
essential light. Significantly, Tauler goes on to say that, if a
man has arrived at this point, he must not let the inferior
powers of his soul remain idle. They must be treated according to their nature, which means in effect, as he makes quite
clear, that the moral virtues must be practised with an ever-

[9] The emphasis laid by the Alexandrian theologians on identification
with the unity and simplicity of God will be recalled. Chap. I, p. 13.

increasing detachment from self. He could not make a more complete rebuttal of any charge of Quietism.

SUSO

Suso also was a Dominican, a disciple of Eckhart, and wrote in German. His strictly mystical teaching is the same as Eckhart's, but he started to write only after the condemnation of his master and is careful to guard against misinterpretation. It is instructive to glance at the content of his work. His first book, *The Little Book of Truth*, is mystical. It treats of union with God through abandonment. The book is written in the form of a dialogue between the disciple (Suso) and Eternal Truth, and though unmethodical, it gives an able exposition of the Dionysian conception of the transcendence of God and the idea of "dark" contemplation. The soul "knows nothing of knowledge, or of love, or of anything whatever. It is entirely and absolutely passive in the Nothing, and knows nothing but being, which is God, or the Nothing. But when it knows and recognizes that it is aware of the Nothing, that it contemplates and knows it, that is a return and a reversion from this highest stage to itself, according to the natural order."[10] The contemplative act is so intense that the soul is completely absorbed, in the psychological sense, in God, and any recognition of its stage at the ordinary level of consciousness means a lessening of the degree of contemplation. The whole work may be said to be a skilful defence of Eckhart, in as much as it puts forward his doctrine while always safeguarding orthodoxy, but in the sixth chapter the dialogue is between the disciple and an unnamed "wild man" (*das namelos Wilde*), and Suso deliberately contrasts his own doctrine with the false abandonment of the Beghards and Brethren of the Free Spirit, even introducing some of Eckhart's condemned propositions, and showing how they are

[10] *Little Book of Truth*, chap. 5, Clark, *op. cit.*, p. 195.

capable of being interpreted in an orthodox manner. His best-known work, *The Little Book of Wisdom*, has nothing mystical in it, but it contains excellent spirituality. The core of the book seems to have been a hundred meditations on the passion, which are summarized at the end, but the leading idea is that of God's love for men and their rejection of him. The work is based on the consideration of Christ in his humanity, but always the reader is led on from the humanity to the divinity, and the emphasis is always on God's love for us as the supreme motive for our love and service of him. There is sorrow for man's rejection of God, and sometimes rather poignant reference to the abuses of an age which was in many ways already preparing for the Reformation, but always there is, as there must be in any true spirituality, stress on conformity to God's will, to abandonment in a general sense, but it is not pushed to the extremes which Eckhart, and all this school in their strictly mystical writings, pushed it, though of course the way was left open. The first degree will be, as he shows in a fine chapter (13), the acceptance of suffering which comes unsought. That is the foundation of the spiritual life. As Suso, following St Gregory, puts it, "patience in suffering is greater than raising the dead or working other miracles". Such an attitude will lead a man to sit lightly to worldly goods and success, for he will accept the loss of them as from the hand of God. That is already a measure of detachment from them, though it is still far from the complete detachment preached by Eckhart, and recognized by Suso too. Psychologically, it would seem, this latter is only possible when a positive desire for the experience of God has been substituted for the desire of earthly things.

We know something of Suso because of his Life,[11] a remarkable document based on a record of conversations with him written down by a nun, Elsbeth Stagel, with extracts

[11] *The Life of the Servant*. Translated by James M. Clark (London, 1952).

from his correspondence; the whole filled out and rewritten by himself. Early in his religious life he went through a period of horrifying bodily austerities which lasted for ten years, but he dropped these and devoted himself to a life obviously of great perfection and charity in the spiritual service of others.

In both Tauler and Suso we find an exclusive method of contemplation, but it is fully integrated into the Christian life, following from the fundamental conformity of the soul to God's will, but not imposed rigidly. There is evidence in his *Talks of Instruction* that the same was true in practice of Eckhart, but he was obviously fascinated by his speculations on the soul's union with God and indulged in them somewhat recklessly. With regard to their own personal experiences Eckhart and Tauler are both very reticent, but Suso in the *Life* admits to having had mystical experiences on a number of occasions, though it is to be noted that the imaginative visions which he described, because they are in the imagination, necessarily do not pertain to the highest contemplation.

RUYSBROECK

In Ruysbroeck we find the fullest and most balanced exposition of this spirituality. He wrote in Flemish and his work, *The Spiritual Espousals* (*De Gheestelike Brulocht*—sometimes translated as *The Adornment of the Spiritual Marriage*) is perhaps the best summary of his teaching.[12] He divides his work into three Books dealing with the active life, what he calls the life of yearning, and the contemplative life, and of these his life of yearning belongs definitely to what is normally called the contemplative state. Overriding this division,

[12] There is an excellent modern English translation, *Jan van Ruysbroek, The Spiritual Espousals* by Eric Colledge (London 1951). Page references below are to this edition. For a shorter exposition of his teaching see *The Seven Steps of the Ladder of Spiritual Love* translated from the Flemish by F. Sherwood Taylor with an introduction by Joseph Bolland, S.J.

though it does not appear till the second Book, is the three-fold unity he finds in man, that is to say, a principle of unification he finds at three levels. To begin with the lowest, there is the unity of his senses by which he lives as an individual on the animal level; above this is the unity of his higher powers, his memory and understanding and will, by which he lives as a rational being, and there is a further and more essential unity that he has in God, in as much as he is dependent on God for his life and the preservation of it, and without this he would fall into nothing. There is an appropriate perfection of man at all three levels in each of the three states of the active, yearning and contemplative lives. Thus in the active life, the life of moral endeavour, which must necessarily be at the basis of Christian spirituality, and which he integrates with his total scheme as the first coming of Christ to the soul, the first unity is supernaturally adorned, in his phrase, by exterior exercises of piety and the effort to achieve moral perfection. In the second unity the supernatural life is manifested in the virtues of faith, hope and charity in the higher powers of the soul. In the third the supernatural action is above our intellectual comprehension and yet is essentially present within us. It is sanctifying grace by which God is united to every soul in a state of grace, but the soul is not conscious of the union as such. The failure to apprehend the union at this stage, of course, is in contrast to the supra-rational apprehension of it in contemplation. But in the attainment of all our union with God the essential distinction is between what he calls union with means and union without means. The means may be external, actual graces conveyed, it may be, through books or sermons; or internal, the recognizable action of God on the soul, the gifts of the Holy Spirit. The first three gifts, fear of the Lord, piety and knowledge, belong to the active life; the other four, fortitude, counsel, understanding and wisdom find their place in the life of yearning, but they are "means", the intellect and will are consciously active. The gift of wisdom is the highest, but in the end we recognize it and savour it for what it is, "we feel this touching in the uniting of our highest powers, above reason, yet not without reason, for we comprehend that we have been touched".[13] But above all this is union without means. This is genuine contemplation, the direct touch of God on the soul, and it occurs in Ruysbroeck's second stage, the life of yearning. "Now understand that God comes ceaselessly to dwell in us by means and without means, and he demands of us both that we enjoy him and that we perform works, and that the one remain unhindered by the other. And thus the inward man possesses his life in these two manners, that is in rest and in action."[14] Ruysbroeck distinguishes between the effect of the Gifts, which is itself incomprehensible at the highest level but which for him is still a union "with means", and the direct touch of union "without means", and both of these occur in his life of yearning.

Above this is an even higher union, which occurs in what he calls the contemplative life proper, and of which he speaks at much less length in the third Book. He is necessarily obscure and he says himself, "No one shall utterly understand the depths of what we now expound by means of any instruction or of any narrow observation of his own".[15] The so-called birth of the Word in the soul takes place. The essence of the soul at its creation is the image of the divine Idea of it, which has existed in God from all eternity. In love the soul goes forth, "in a loving flowing-out, in darkness and lacking all manner. There the spirit is embraced in the Holy Trinity, eternally remaining in the super-essential unity in rest and delectation."[16] This highest union consists in a sort of return of the soul to the divine exemplar. When he reaches the very height of his perfection, man returns to his point of departure, to his uncreated being existing in the divine Essence. The soul

[13] Bk. II, chap. XXXIV, p. 160.
[14] Bk. II, chap. XXXVIII, p. 165.
[15] Bk. III, Introduction, pp. 179–80.
[16] Bk. III, chap. VI, p. 185.

loses, in some way, its existence to become the divine idea according to which it was created, and yet Ruysbroeck is insistent that the soul is not identified with God, and does not lose its personality. Such are the speculations into which Ruysbroeck is led in his attempt to describe the highest union. The limits of human thought and language are reached, but it should be said that Ruysbroeck has never seriously been accused of unorthodoxy, and he has in fact been beatified by the Church.

THE ENGLISH MYSTICS

During this same fourteenth century a group of spiritual writers in the vernacular arose in England who are generally known as the fourteenth-century English mystics. Essentially they belong to the same school of spirituality as the Rhineland and Flemish writers we have been studying, but it would not seem that they derive directly from them. Late in the century some of Ruysbroeck's works were translated and made use of,[17] but the movement seems rather to have run parallel to the contemporary one on the Continent, and like that owed its chief literary inspiration to the pseudo-Denis. If England suffered less from political upheavals at this time, it was permeated by very much the same intellectual atmosphere, and this, it must be supposed, produced the tendency to seek an experimental form of religion. At any rate the tendency is well illustrated by the earliest of these writers, Richard Rolle.

RICHARD ROLLE

Rolle's writings are not important for the contribution which they make to spiritual literature, but they tell us a

[17] Eight out of twenty-seven chapters of *The Chastising of God's Children* are translated, with omissions, from a Latin translation of *The Spiritual Espousals*. Another small work *The Treatise of Perfection of the Sons of God* is a translation of a Latin version of Ruysbroeck's treatise of the same name. The latter is included in the recent edition of the *Chastising* by J. Bazire and E. Colledge.

good deal about himself,[18] and his life is of great interest as illustrating the spontaneous desire for contemplation which seems to have been a feature of his times, and which of itself must have done much to elicit the literature with which we are dealing. He left Oxford as a student, and soon afterwards ran away from home to become a sort of free-lance hermit, and in one of his works, the *Incendium Amoris*[19] (chap. 15), he describes how during the first five years of his eremitical career he was the recipient of various mystical experiences. He experienced in prayer, and it would seem the experiences became habitual, what he describes as *calor*, *dulcor* and *canor* —heat, sweetness and song. There is no space to discuss here what he meant by these, but there seems no doubt that the first and last at any rate were felt in the senses and it is, of course, well known that mystical experiences may react on the body. He wrote in both English and Latin, and the chronology of his works cannot be fixed exactly, but it is possible, nevertheless, to trace his spiritual development quite clearly from the internal evidence of his writings. The independent, and apparently rather roving, hermit's life which he had adopted was likely to cause criticism, and there is evidence that he himself did not hesitate to criticize others. A work in which he refers to himself as a youth, the *Judica me Deus*, is largely taken up with criticism of the clergy. No doubt the fourteenth-century clergy merited a good deal of criticism, but they would certainly resent it from a young man in Rolle's position, and the whole of a very curious work called the *Melos Contemplativorum* is really a defence of

[18] After his death an Office was composed by the nuns of Hampole, with whom he was in close association at the end of his life, in anticipation of his canonization, which never took place. The Nocturn lessons tell the story of his life, and are probably good evidence for the external facts. The canon of his works has been satisfactorily established and much information gathered about him by Miss Emily Allen in *Writings ascribed to Richard Rolle and materials for his biography* (London, 1927).

[19] Latin edition by Margaret Deansley (Manchester, 1915). English translation, *The Fire of Love and the Mending of Life*, by Frances Comper (London, 1914).

himself and the way of life he had adopted. It is human to resent criticism of one's actions, but it is one of the surest signs of sanctity to be able to take it without resentment. He would have done better not to justify himself in writing at all, but to have let his life be its own ultimate justification. The recent editor of the *Melos*[20] adopts a very generous and charitable attitude to Rolle in his Introduction, but when all is said that can be in his favour, the fact remains that not only did he defend himself, but he did it very intemperately, for a contemplative! He expresses the conventional regard for humility, but he did not manifest the virtue. The exaggerated alliteration of the Latin prose—it must be unique in this respect—in itself produces an effect of nervous excitement, which is not the ideal state in which such a work, if it had to have been written at all, should have been produced. It is a question, too, as to whether it was really a high degree of contemplation that he valued at this stage of his religious life, and not a mere sensible accompaniment, and the way in which he always refers to the external phenomena raises a suspicion. The point is important, because there is a real danger in surrender to the sensible pleasure which may accompany experiences of this sort. It is not surprising that Rolle should have shown a certain intemperateness, because he lacked precisely that training which the cenobitic life he so despised was designed to give. Heat, sound and sweetness, whatever form they may have taken, are, of course, no more than possible concomitants of mystical experience, and they do not accompany the highest sort. On the other hand, there can be no question but that Rolle was perfectly sincere in his turning to God, and that he received the grace of some high degree of prayer. The fact that physical concomitants played such a large part would be a temperamental peculiarity of his own—not unique, not wrong, but dangerous. He did not really

[20] Dr E. J. F. Arnould, *The Melos Amoris of Richard Rolle of Hampole*. This is the first time the *Melos* has been printed, and all students of Rolle must be grateful to Dr Arnould for a scholarly edition of this important work.

get off to a very good start in his religious life, but that his view of it deepened considerably is shown in other works, which may therefore be presumed to be later than the *Melos*. In the *Incendium Amoris* he is much more temperate. He condemns sin in others, but objectively not personally. He is learning to hate the sin and love the sinner. He is still a little sensitive to criticism, but even if he feels some slight resentment, he realizes the ideal to be aimed at. The spiritual man must be ready to suffer wrongs: "If you find your soul unprepared to suffer wrongs or death, you show that you are not God's true lover" (chap. 10). In a diffuse and wandering book there is much sound traditional teaching on the spiritual life, and if references to much of it could probably be found in the *Melos*, the atmosphere is totally different. The shrill notes of self-justification are toned down, and for the most part Rolle no longer holds himself up as an example of the virtues.

His other important works are the *Emendatio Vitae*[21] in Latin, and three short treatises, generally referred to as the *Epistles*,[22] in English. Here we have something different. He is a teacher and authority, no longer concerned to justify his position. But it is to be noted that his writings in themselves hardly belong to the school we are dealing with. He himself may be said to belong to the spiritual movement which was taking place on the Continent and in England, because of his interest in and desire for contemplation, but he shows none of the speculative interest in the nature of the act that was characteristic of Eckhart and Ruysbroeck. He seems to know nothing of the Dionysian approach that was described in such detail by the author of *The Cloud of Unknowing*, and the authorities that he quotes in his later works belong to the older tradition in Western Europe. It is interesting that the mystical experiences about which in the earlier works he

[21] Translated as *The Mending of Life* along with *The Fire of Love* by Frances Comper, *op. cit.*

[22] Available in *Richard Rolle, English Writings* edited by Hope Emily Allen (Oxford, 1931).

talked so much, and in a sense said so little, do not figure very largely in the later writings. He is concerned with laying foundations, and he has grasped that these must be interior rather than exterior. The *Emendatio* is perhaps the most valuable of all his works. It is an admirable exposition of traditional teaching, and there is more warmth about it than about the English *Epistles*. Any doubts about his attitude to the sensible joys of contemplation are dispelled. "In this degree or state of love is love chaste, holy, willing; loving the Beloved for himself alone, not for his gifts."[23] In these later treatises Rolle makes use freely of ordered categories, many of which are traceable to known sources. It is an implicit commentary on his own earlier views. Even in the *Incendium* he is still scornful of the learned. The humble contemplative, he says, shall be taught with wisdom from on high, "but those taught by wisdom acquired not inshed, and those swollen with folded arguments, will disdain him saying, 'Where did he learn? Under what doctor did he sit?' For they do not admit that the lovers of eternity are taught by a doctor from within to speak more eloquently than they themselves, who have learned from men, and studied all the time for empty honours."[24] In these English works he is often demonstrably indebted to standard authors, too much perhaps. It is rather touching after his previous attitude. He has certainly come a long way from the time when he wrote the *Melos*. His very willingness to recognize the authority of others has added to his own authority, and if he has lost something in romantic appeal, he has gained, perhaps, a more solid title to fame.

THE CLOUD OF UNKNOWING

The author of *The Cloud of Unknowing* (he is still unidentified) is a notable exponent of the pure Dionysian doctrine. He states in the Prologue that he is writing for those

[23] Chap 11.   [24] Bk. II, chap. 3.

who aim at being perfect followers of Christ, and that not merely by the practice of good works but precisely through contemplation. It is a good example of the new attitude, the cult of contemplation. For such a one he gives explicit instruction on how to set about his task. But the instruction is very specialized. He takes the whole background of the "practical" life, the interior practice of virtue, for granted. But within the framework of the religious life as known and understood at the time—and it would include the eremitical —a man who wants to practise contemplation must carry out a definite exercise for several hours a day. He does not say how many, but implies a lot. The book consists of careful instructions as to how this exercise, which the author always refers to as the "work", is to be carried out. On the Dionysian principle that contemplation is something supra-intellectual it is his contention that the work of the intellect can only hinder it. The exercise will, therefore, consist in concentrating the mind on the simplest idea of God (there must be something to concentrate it), and rigidly excluding all thought of everything created—all images. It is the abandonment of Eckhart. But there must be desire for God, what he calls the "naked intent of the will to God".

> This darkness and this cloud, howsoever thou dost, is betwixt thee and thy God, and hindereth thee, so that thou mayest neither see him clearly by light of understanding in thy reason, nor feel him in sweetness of love in thine affection. And therefore shape thee to bide in this darkness as long as thou mayest, evermore crying after him whom thou lovest. For if ever thou shalt see him or feel him, as it may be here, it must always be in this cloud and in this darkness. And if thou wilt busily travail as I bid thee, I trust in his mercy that thou shalt come thereto (chap. 3, p. 8).[25]

The initial human effort of concentration does not, of course, constitute the contemplation, but the author believes

[25] Page references are to the sixth and revised edition (1952) in the Orchard Series by Dom Justin McCann.

that to one who has arrived at the proper dispositions God will give this formless knowledge. As Hilton will tell us, it is sometimes comforting, sometimes painful, sometimes illuminated by rays of divine light, but with this the author of the *Cloud* does not concern himself. He confines himself strictly to what the soul must do in order to enter this *cloud of unknowing*. There is no question but the experience is the work of God, though a man do what he can to further it. "And, therefore lift up thy love to that cloud. Or rather (if I shall say thee sooth) let God draw thy love up to that cloud; and strive thou through help of his grace to forget all other things" (chap. 9, p. 21). The process will be difficult at the beginning, but afterwards it will become easier, "for then will God work sometimes all by himself. But not always so, nor yet a long time together, but when he liketh and as he liketh; and then wilt thou think it merry to let him alone" (chap. 26, p. 43). ". . . it is the work of only God specially wrought in whatever soul he liketh, without any merit of the same soul. . . . It is neither given for innocence, nor withholden for sin" (chap. 34, pp. 48–9). Nevertheless, to one earnestly seeking it he believes it will be granted. "If thou wilt busily travail as I bid thee, I trust in his mercy that thou shalt come thereto" (chap. 3, p. 8). The basis of the process is to be the undistracted focusing of the attention on the simple Being of God.

> And therefore, when thou purposest thee to this work . . . lift up thy heart unto God with a meek stirring of love. And mean God that made thee, and bought thee, and that graciously hath called thee to thy degree; and receive none other thought of God. And yet not all these, except thou desirest; for a naked intent directed unto God, without any other cause than himself, sufficeth wholly. And if thou desirest to have this intent lapped and folden in one word, so that thou mayest have better hold thereupon, take thee but a little word of one syllable, for so it is better than of two (chap. 7, p. 16).

And he suggests just the word GOD or LOVE. There is to be no discursive reasoning, no inward discussion of the subject. Even thoughts about God and the saints are a distraction. "Yea—and if it be courteous and seemly to say—in this work it profiteth little or nought to think of the kindness or worthiness of God, nor on our Lady, nor on the saints and angels in heaven" (chap. 5, pp. 13–4). Even meditation on the passion of Christ will lead a man to think of his sins, and that will recall details of his past life, "so that at the last, ere ever thou knowest, thou shalt be scattered thou knowest not where". But he is emphatic that there is no coming to contemplation unless such meditations have been made, "and yet, a man or woman that hath long time been practised in these meditations, must nevertheless leave them, and put them and hold them far down under the *cloud of forgetting* if ever he shall pierce the *cloud of unknowing* betwixt him and his God" (chap. 7, p. 16). It is not that thoughts of the goodness of God, or of his personal goodness to us, are wrong. "Nay, God forbid that thou take it so. But I say that although it be good and holy, yet in this work it hindereth more than it profiteth" (chap. 9, p. 21). He makes it clear that it is God who is to be sought and not an experience. The substance of the work is the naked intent of the will directed to God for himself, "because in this work a perfect prentice asketh neither releasing of pain, nor increasing of reward, nor (shortly to say) naught but himself" (chap. 24, p. 40). The author of the *Cloud*, it has been said, will concern himself with no more than what may be called the basic attainment of contemplation, and the statement is not contradicted by his only reference to possible further experiences. "Then will he (God) sometimes peradventure send out a beam of ghostly light, piercing this *cloud of unknowing* that is betwixt thee and him, and show thee some of his secrets, the which man may not and cannot speak. . . . For of that work that pertaineth only to God dare I not take upon me to speak with my blabbering fleshly tongue" (chap. 26, p. 43). Of the more recondite aspects of the subject, which so occupied Eckhart and Ruysbroeck, he will say nothing, though he was aware of their existence. He mentions other points which are commonly treated by authors of this school, and his teaching coincides with that invariably given. The practice of contemplation has in itself a purifying effect on the character. This is the result, it seems in fact, of the gifts of the Holy Spirit, which are given in a more abundant measure, and whose proper effect is precisely to facilitate the practice of virtue. The two virtues which are always the surest signs of a high degree of grace are humility and charity, and he distinguishes, as is customary, between the humility which comes as the result of a man's own efforts of observation and integrity, and that which comes as the result of contemplation. Through this a man comes to some sort of realization of what the goodness of God means, "and in this time it is perfectly meeked, for it knoweth and feeleth no cause but the chief" (chap. 13, p. 26). This is humility of an altogether deeper kind. He advocates a great discretion in matters of food and drink and sleep, maintaining that one who pursues his exercise will certainly be guided in these matters, and implying that he will not be called to adopt practices of exceptional severity. Finally, at some length he warns against an unwise pursuit of contemplation (chaps. 45, 46, 51–7). We have seen that on the Continent there was a good deal of cause for this. The author of the *Cloud* must have been aware of the extreme dangers of perfectionism and antinomianism, but he seems to have had more immediately in mind the danger that the sort of concentration that he advocated would produce some sort of effect akin to hypnosis—and there can be little doubt that the danger existed.

WALTER HILTON

Walter Hilton, who died in 1395, was an Augustinian canon, though it is probable that he only became one late in life. Practically nothing is known with certainty about his early life, but he was the author of one major work in English and a number of smaller ones in both Latin and English. *The Scale of Perfection* is by far his most important work, and it is a remarkable and valuable treatise on the whole spiritual life. It was written for an anchoress, and Hilton takes it for granted that the object of her life is to strive for contemplation. In this respect he has exactly the same attitude as the author of the *Cloud*, and it was, as we have seen, characteristic of the school to which they belonged. Hilton, perhaps because he had had a wide experience of life, takes a comprehensive view of spirituality, and he treats it with some originality, but it was still contemplation that he saw as the goal, and he describes it as the restoration of the image of God in man. He calls it the reforming—he uses the word in a technical sense, and it seems better to keep it—of this image.[26] Before the Fall man was in the image of God in the sense that the three powers of his soul, memory, understanding and will, were directed primarily to God, but as the result of Adam's sin man fell from this state "into forgetfulness and ignorance of God, and into a monstrous love of himself" (I, 43; p. 64).[27] As a result of the passion and death of Christ man may be restored to the image of God, in the sense in which he has used the term, fully only in heaven, but partially here on earth. Into this partial restoration Hilton introduces a further distinction. It may be in faith only, or in faith and feeling. A man is restored to the image of God in faith only, when he is simply in a state of grace, but he is restored in faith and feeling, when he is not merely in a state of grace, but when by the power of the Holy Ghost he is aware of the working of grace in him (II, 5; p. 154). The attainment of this state is the proper object of the contemplative life. The teaching is important and valuable, because it brings out the idea of

[26] The *Scale* consists of two Books of which the second, while recapitulating the doctrine of the first, fills it out, particularly with regard to contemplation. He treats of reforming the image of God in man in both Books I, 42–5, and II, 1–20.

[27] Page references are to the modern English version in the second Orchard Series (1953).

contemplation as an awareness of the life of grace. "The soul understands something of what it knew before only by faith" (II, 33; p. 246). The soul's happiness consists in this knowledge, and it is the presence in the soul of Uncreated Love, that is the Holy Spirit, which brings it about (II, 34; p. 248).

Such is the way in which Hilton fits contemplation into the spiritual life, but it does not emerge until the second half of the second Book of the *Scale*. In the first Book (46–54) he describes the means by which contemplation is to be attained. It is fundamentally by desire for God, "for Jesus, it is all the same", he says (I, 46; p. 73). This must always be the foundation of the process. It is "the naked intent of the will unto God" of *The Cloud of Unknowing*, but in this connection Hilton goes on to give some valuable practical advice which may quite properly be applied to souls on a much lower level than those he had in view. We are to seek God within ourselves, he says, but the first effort to do this will be disappointing. We shall find, not the image of God for which we were looking, but what he calls the "image of sin". We shall become aware of our own shortcomings, and beyond that, of what he calls the roots of sin in us, the latent capacity for evil which is in all men. It is a valuable experience, and indeed a necessary one. Many who are making a serious effort to lead a spiritual life meet it, and think it is a bad sign, but it is a good one. It means that the real work of turning to God has at least begun. When we have discovered these evil tendencies within us, we have to eradicate them so far as may be, and Hilton devotes no less than thirty-eight chapters to the process (I, 55–92). Such is the foundation he lays for the spiritual life of his contemplative. Granted that the contemplative life has begun in this way, Hilton describes its course by two images, that of a pilgrimage to Jerusalem (II, 21), and that of the passage through the night (II, 24). To take the second first; the night, he says, lies between two days, the day of this world's love and the day of the perfect love of Jesus. The true light of the second day comes to us only in heaven, but we have to go through the night in order to reach it. There is no doubt, it would seem, that the night he is referring to is the *cloud of unknowing*. It is in it that the partial reform in faith and feeling, which is contemplation, the awareness of grace, will be attained. Sometimes the night will be distressing, for the attractions of the world will still be felt, but gradually the soul will come to rest in it, and "Jesus, who is both love and light, is in the darkness whether it is distressing or peaceful" (II, 24; p. 207). A pilgrimage suggests itself easily enough as an image of the spiritual life, but the lesson which Hilton wants to drive home by it, and he does so in some vivid prose, is the necessity for determination in pursuing the way regardless of difficulties. He gives what has become since the introduction of the Dionysian spirituality the normal teaching on the necessity for transcending the imagination (II, 30 and 33), but he is a good deal less clear about the part the intellect may play. He mentions the effect of contemplation in producing humility (II, 37) and the other virtues. "Love brings all virtues into the soul and makes them agreeable and pleasant . . . for the soul does not struggle to attain them as it did before, but it possesses them easily and rests in them through this gift of Love" (II, 36; p. 258). Out of his two lengthy Books he devotes only three chapters to the sensible concomitants of contemplation, such as visions (II, 44–6). Again in accordance with the tradition of this school, he is very moderate in what he has to say about food and drink and sleep and bodily penance. Mortification for him is chiefly internal, destroying the roots of sin. There is wisdom and understanding and sympathy in all that Hilton writes, and although he is giving explicit instruction in the contemplative life for one he believes ought to pursue it, he has a good deal to say about those who by the terms of his own definition have not attained it (II, 1–20). Nor does he underrate this state—of reform in faith alone—in which "the majority of God's elect lead their lives".

JULIAN OF NORWICH

Julian of Norwich is one of that not inconsiderable band of women who have played an important part in the history of Christian mysticism. The recipient of unusual favours and experiences, she is obviously balanced, humble, wise and charitable; marked off by all the gifts of character and grace necessary to prove the genuineness of her claims. In her only book, *The Revelations of Divine Love,* she comes forward not as a teacher and master providing a map and general information for those setting out to explore a country for themselves, or anxious only to learn about it, but as a traveller returned with a first-hand description of what she has seen there. Visions and other psycho-physical phenomena have played little part in this history of spirituality, because the masters of that science have always regarded them as, at the best, no more than by-products of mystical experience, with the possibility always in mind that they may be dangerous wills-o'-the-wisp; for the old writers products of the devil *tout simple,* for the modern ones of psychological disorder. But those who have penetrated far into this country have perhaps always encountered them, and none bear the marks of grace more distinctly than Julian's. She tells us in her *Revelations* that she had a series of visions on May 8th, 1373. Fifteen occurred between four and nine in the morning, and one more the following night. For the latter part of her life she was certainly an anchoress in Norwich, but in what state of life she was when she had the visions is uncertain. The circumstances she describes, the presence of her mother and the parish-priest, suggest they occurred in her own home. At any rate it is certain that she was already living an intense spiritual life, for she tells us that in the past she had prayed for three things, remembrance of the passion of Christ, a sickness when she should be thirty years of age, and what she called three wounds, namely contrition, compassion and desire for God. She had forgotten, she tells us, the first two requests, but when she was thirty the sickness came upon her, and at the climax of it the visions occurred. As described by her they were partly imaginative (or corporeal) of the passion of Christ, partly intellectual, that is intellectual illuminations or intuitions, partly, it would seem, merging from one into the other. There are two versions of her *Revelations,* a longer and a shorter, both, there is every reason to believe, genuine. She tells us that in the twenty years following her visions, she had further light on them, and the longer version of her book contains apparently the results of this further illumination. The outcome is a very remarkable body of spiritual teaching. It is not that she has anything technical to say about contemplation, though her experiences have all been equated with what has come to be considered the classical teaching on the subject. It is possible that she had never heard of the writings attributed to Denis the Areopagite. It may be that she never experienced the most profound mystical state. Her visions would properly belong to something less exalted, but although she claimed to be unlearned—she "could no letter" she says—she has left a spirituality more soundly based on dogmatic theology than most.

It will perhaps be best to consider here just one point which embodies her real message. Running through all Julian's reflections on her experiences is a twofold theme, which is sometimes more in evidence, sometimes less, until it emerges as dominant in the final chapters. We have, she says, "matter of mirth, and matter of moaning; matter of mirth, for our Lord, our Maker, is so near to us, and in us, and we in him, by sureness of keeping through his great goodness; matter of moaning, for our ghostly eye is so blind and we be so borne down by weight of our mortal flesh and darkness of sin, that we may not see our Lord clearly in his fair Blissful Cheer" (72, p. 146).[28] That is the expression of two great truths which must always form the basis of the spiritual life.

[28] Page references are to the second Orchard Series edition (1952), *Revelations of Divine Love.*

That we have matter for moaning hardly needs emphasis. "It behoveth us verily to see that of ourselves we are right naught but sin and wretchedness" (chap. 28, p. 158). But what we must never lose sight of is that God dwells in us, and we in him, if we are in a state of grace.

> Highly ought we to rejoice that God dwelleth in our soul, and much more highly ought we to rejoice that our soul dwelleth in God. Our soul is made to be God's dwelling-place, and the dwelling-place of the soul is God, which is unmade. And high understanding it is inwardly to see and know that God, which is our Maker, dwelleth in our soul; and a higher understanding it is inwardly to see and know that our soul, that is made, dwelleth in God's substance; of which substance, God, we are what we are. (54. p. 110.)

It is surely of the greatest importance to realize that that is true not only of the soul enjoying contemplative union, but of every soul in grace. The contemplative has an awareness of the grace, at least in its effects, as Hilton said, and this will admit of an infinite number of degrees, and it is not really important to try and assess the exact degree of awareness. In at least one other passage Julian is equally explicit on this indwelling of God (chap. 67, p. 139). All the time she stresses the fact that God gives himself to man in this way as a result of his own goodness, and not because there is anything in man which could merit such a gift. It is her emphasis on these great truths which makes Julian's message so inspiring, but it also led her into certain difficulties. She lays so much emphasis on the soul's union with God that she says apparently on two occasions that it cannot be broken. In chapter 37 (p. 65) she says, "for in every soul that shall be saved is a Godly Will that never assented unto sin, nor ever shall", and in chapter 59 (p. 122), "For in him (the Second Person) we have the Godly Will whole and safe without end." Theologians are apt to make rather heavy weather of these statements, it would seem because they take them at their face value as theological propositions. But we can perhaps get a clearer idea of what she was trying to say, if we examine another statement of her general thesis in chapter 52. "All that shall be saved, we have in us for the time of this life, a marvellous medley both of weal and woe: we have in us our Lord Jesus uprisen, we have in us the wretchedness and the mischief of Adam's falling and dying" (p. 103). She goes on to describe how the soul is alternately refreshed by Christ, and then apparently overwhelmed by the weakness of its fallen nature. "But then is this our comfort, that we know in our faith that by virtue of Christ which is our Keeper, we assent never thereto, but we grudge there against, and endure in pain and woe, unto that time that he showeth him again to us" (p. 104). It is a very good description of anyone trying to lead the spiritual life, and it finds its explanation precisely in the twofold theme which we have examined as being Julian's essential message; the soul realizes, with greater or less distinctness, now God's goodness, now its own sinfulness. And when she says that this is our comfort in tribulation, that "we know in our faith that by virtue of Christ which is our keeper, we assent never thereto", she is not intending to propound a theological thesis; she is only saying that a soul which is seriously seeking God will feel deep down, even under the most violent temptations or in the bleakest desolation, that it is not separated from God. It is the "little secret trust" which Hilton says will be left to the soul, even when the storm is at its worst. In this same chapter she is perfectly realistic about the place of sin in human life.

Notwithstanding all this, I saw and understood in our Lord's meaning that we may not in this life keep us from sin as wholly in full cleanness as we shall be in Heaven ... and we go forthwith to God in love; and neither, on the one side, fall over-low, inclining to despair, nor on the other side, be over-reckless as if we made no matter of it; but nakedly acknowledging our feebleness, (we) wit that we may not stand the twinkling of an eye but by keeping of grace, and reverently cleave to God, on him only trusting (p. 105).

This is the solution of her difficulty in reconciling her revelations, in which God does not appear to attach blame to man, with the teaching of the Church concerning sin and its punishment (45–50). Julian's writings are very precious. What we should like to know is her spiritual history before she had the revelations, and what direction she received. It has been pointed out that evidently she had already progressed some way in the spiritual life but we just know nothing about her earlier circumstances.

SUMMARY

Richard Rolle and Julian of Norwich, though in a general way they are clearly to be connected with the movement we are considering in this chapter, are rather special cases, but the two fourteenth-century English mystics who *ex professo* gave instruction in the subject are in marked contrast to the continental mystics, especially Eckhart and Ruysbroeck. Fundamentally they were teaching the same doctrine, but the latter were speculative, interested in trying to analyse and define the nature of the soul's union with God. They were practical too, but the English writers were wholly so. Whether this was to be attributed to their national temperament, which for the most part is not given to abstract speculation, is an open question, but the fact remains and is very striking. There is no doubt that the movement was less widespread in England than it was on the Continent. We hear nothing in this country of sects such as the Beghards and the Brethren of the Free Spirit, who succumbed wholesale to the dangers inherent in an unwise pursuit of contemplation. Nevertheless the movement must have been sufficiently widespread in England to make the authorities aware of the dangers. This is undoubtedly the reason for the suspicions aroused by Margery Kempe,[29] and the trials to which she was subjected. She was a

[29] *The Book of Margery Kempe*, a modern version by W. Butler-Bowden (London, 1936).

lay-woman of King's Lynn who, while she may have been the recipient of genuinely mystical experiences, certainly re-acted to them in a violently emotional way, though she appears always to have remained perfectly orthodox. It is to be noted that the treatise called *The Chastising of God's Children*,[30] which gives warning of the difficulties, and indeed afflictions, which may overtake the contemplative, is only in part concerned with the dangers of false mysticism. Much of it describes the temptations and aridities which are likely to come to all those who make a serious attempt to pursue holiness, and which are good signs rather than bad ones.

If it seems to us that the intellectual speculations of Eckhart and Ruysbroeck are very fine-spun and abstract. We should remember that they have a long history. It was inevitable that the first Christian thinkers, brought up in the intellectual *milieu* in which they were, should have occupied themselves deeply with the problem of man's union with God, and if Christianity shows a wonderful balance between the spiritual and the incarnational, it would seem to have been in the designs of Providence that there should have been this in-fusion of ideas, and without them Catholic theology could not have developed.

There is no doubt that the speculations of the fourteenth-century school threw light on the true nature of contempla-tion. They established that it is the direct action of God on the soul, which transcends all the natural faculties. It is the work of God, and we are not to believe that this work only began in the fourteenth century, but the earlier medieval writers did not define it so accurately, and they used the term contemplation, as did many of those who came after them, to describe the action of grace on the soul which yet fell short of the full contemplative experience. The action of God on chosen souls is, of course, something to be approached

---

[30] *The Chastising of God's Children and the Treatise of Perfection of the Sons of God* edited from the Manuscripts by Joyce Bazire and Eric Colledge (Oxford, 1957).

with great reverence, and for that very reason anything suggesting a deliberate attempt to cultivate it makes one a little uneasy, and there is an element of that about all these writers. Perhaps it was inevitable in the spiritual atmosphere of the fourteenth century, poles apart as they were from the quite manifestly false mysticism rife on parts of the Continent. In the case of these theologians, too, it may be that they were affected, perhaps unconsciously, by faint echoes of the Neo-Platonic conception of the "contemplative life" which they found in their sources.

CHAPTER IV

THE FIFTEENTH CENTURY

The school of mysticism which had in Ruysbroeck such a profound representative was, of course, independent of the vagaries of popular mysticism. It continued, and in the Franciscan Hendrik Herp († 1477), generally known as Harphius, the Latinized form of his name, it had another notable exponent. Later it was to spread out into the great Spanish and French schools. But there was, nevertheless, a certain reaction against it at the end of the fourteenth century which manifested itself at two levels. On the one hand it consisted in the development by the most influential spiritual writers of the day of an affective, empirical, spirituality, whose chief concern was to ensure a firm foundation by laying stress on the initial and fundamental turning to God, and on the fight against the weakness of human nature. It was the spirituality which found its fullest expression in the *Imitation of Christ*. But there was also opposition to mysticism among the theologians of the University of Paris. Two of its chancellors, Peter d'Ailly and John Gerson, felt it incumbent on them to give warning against the excesses and extravagances of false mysticism, and their action in this respect was timely and necessary. But for them a further difficulty arose from the fact that it is nearly always possible to find passages in writers such as Ruysbroeck which as they stand can be objected to by a theologian. But the isolation of such passages never does justice to the author, whose orthodoxy on general grounds may be assured, and their negative criticism of this nature was not really satisfactory.

THE IMITATION OF CHRIST

It is a commonplace of history that there was need for widespread reform in the Church by the end of the fourteenth century, though this is not the place to discuss the causes or examine the needs in detail. No doubt there was much which could only be brought about from above, the whole machinery of Church government was in need of overhaul, and this was something which had to wait for the Council of Trent more than a hundred and fifty years later. But no amount of overhauling machinery could by itself bring about the change which was needed. What was wanted was a fundamental renovation of Christian life. The outward forms were never more developed or strongly entrenched, but to a great extent the spirit had gone out of them. It was not merely that there was lack of enthusiasm; basic principles were being questioned. The possibility of supporting faith and revelation by reason was being denied, and the schools had become no more than a path to academic and political promotion.[1] And if the foundations were being sapped, the pillars which supported the external life of the Church were being shaken too. For example Wyclif in the late fourteenth century was calling in question the justification of the whole religious life in its technical sense, the life of the three vows, and when Gerson wrote a treatise on clerical celibacy in 1413, he was able to quote many opinions demanding its suppression. For the most part, however, the old ideals were still upheld in theory, but they were betrayed in practice. What was needed was a renewal of spiritual life in the Church, a renewal which had to begin with the fundamental conversion of the individual. This was a need which was going to be felt increasingly as the Renaissance got under way, and we shall have to examine

---

[1] The attitude of the *Imitation* towards learning has often been noticed. "What good do you get by disputing learnedly about the Trinity, if you are lacking in humility and are therefore displeasing to the Trinity?" (I, I, 3), and much more to the same effect. It is a commentary on the condition of the schools.

the steps which were beginning to be taken at the end of our period, and which were to be developed more fully later on, to meet the new needs.

But already at the end of the fourteenth century the challenge was being met. The process began in the Low Countries when Gerard Groot (1340–84), a typical rich, worldly, ecclesiastic was "converted" in the year 1370. Others of like mind gathered round him, and the Brethren of the Common Life were formed at Deventer. This was the start of a reform of which the monastery of Windesheim soon became the focal point.[2] We are well informed about the early days through contemporary chronicles and Lives,[3] and there is no doubt that the movement was a direct and spontaneous response to the need which was felt for a renovation of the Christian life. The Brethren of the Common Life gave themselves at first to the copying of manuscripts, and later to the running of schools, through which they had an important influence on the history of education. They also preached and wrote, and their influence spread through the multiplication of their houses in the Low Countries and Germany. A number of their writings are still extant, but they have all been overshadowed by the one great work which the movement produced, *The Imitation of Christ*. It is generally attributed to Thomas à Kempis (1380–1471), though even now the attribution is not absolutely certain, but in any case there is no doubt that the book emanated from the Brethren of the Common Life and represents their spirituality.

The concrete, practical manner of the *Imitation* is well

[2] The Brethren of the Common Life had at first no vows, but Groot's successor, Florent Radewijns, founded the monastery at Windesheim under the rule of the Canons Regular of St Augustine, and it was under this rule inspired by a new spirit that the Congregation of Windesheim was formed and came to exercise a great influence. The name Brethren of the Common Life was often applied to the whole movement.

[3] In English are available by Thomas à Kempis *The Chronicle of the Canons Regular of Mount St Agnes*, translated by J. P. Arthur (London, 1906), and *The Founders of the New Devotion* translated by J. P. Arthur (London, 1905).

known. The teaching is put forward almost in the form of maxims, though the matter, of course, was not new. The book gives very much the same basic presentation of Christianity that was to be found in the anonymous tracts of the Middle Ages already referred to, but the world of Thomas à Kempis had great need of having its attention drawn to such basic teaching. Europe was nominally Christian, and there were, of course, as there always are, devout souls, but they were not so much in evidence as the large numbers of relaxed and worldly clergy and indifferent lay-folk, while of those who had religious interests many tended to an unbalanced and undisciplined religiosity. That a book such as the *Imitation* could make a successful appeal to a world of this sort is a witness to the innate strength of Christianity, of the power of the Church to renew itself from within, in the last analysis to the grace of God. Throughout, the *Imitation* presupposes that its reader has faith, and in presuming this of his contemporaries the author was no doubt right. Faith was still there, though it had much need of being activated. Starting from this premiss, what the *Imitation* does in the first place is to put forward motives for turning to God, and relentlessly the author stresses the little happiness that is to be found in worldliness, and the danger that the worldly soul runs of incurring eternal misery. It has to be admitted that throughout the *Imitation*, and especially in the first two Books, there is heavy emphasis on this negative aspect. It is the theme of renunciation, of giving up the pursuit of riches and worldly honour. But the negative approach by itself is, of course, fruitless. If there is to be renunciation of the world it must be for God. Giving up the world and turning to God must be as it were two sides of the same coin. To take up one is to take up the other. And external renunciation is not enough, it is only a beginning. There must be internal renunciation, detachment from the things of this world, and more important and more far-reaching there must be renunciation of self-will. The author of the *Imitation* has a good deal to say about this, for example in Book III, chapter 11, "That the desires of the heart are to be examined and controlled", or in the following chapter on "Patience", and again in an admirable chapter (Bk. III, chap. 37), "Of a pure and entire resignation of ourselves for the obtaining freedom of heart", but even here perhaps it is a legitimate criticism to say that the approach is a little negative. The necessity for resignation is urged and its fruits extolled, but little is done, here or elsewhere, to show *how* self-love and self-seeking is the root of all sin and the cause of our unhappiness. Detachment from the very thought of created things was, as we have seen, the basic demand of the fourteenth-century mystics, but the author of the *Imitation* is concerned with a more elementary and, in a way, a more fundamental detachment. We are living in the world surrounded by created things, but the cause of our trouble is our desire to impose our will on them, to mould all that surrounds us, people and things, to our own desire.

It is in the third Book that the author turns to the obverse of renunciation, the attainment of friendship with Christ. There is much aspiration, but it is true to say that always the thought turns back to the sinful and impotent individual. In a sense no language can be exaggerated in the expression of this, and without a doubt the whole work is coloured by the desire to preach repentance to a generation which seemed in especial need of it. But the next stage is surely one in which this can, not indeed be forgotten, but in a sense transcended, when, taking our misery for granted, we can look more at our Lord than at ourselves. If the author was Thomas à Kempis, we know from other books that he wrote that he was not unaware of this, and indeed there is constant reference to it, but his preoccupation is always to recall sinful man to the remembrance of his condition.

In the fourth Book the author repeats the ideas of Book III with reference to the Eucharist. He accepts, of course, the practice of the time with regard to Holy Communion, "How happy is he and how acceptable to God, who lives so good a life and keeps his conscience so pure, that he is prepared and well disposed to communicate every day, were it permitted to him and were he able to do so without attracting too much notice" (Bk. IV, chap. 1, 5), but the stress he lays on receiving our Lord in the Blessed Sacrament is very striking, "Thou commandest me to approach to thee with confidence, if I would have part with thee; and to receive the food of immortality, if I desire to obtain everlasting life and glory. *Come to me,* sayest thou, *all you that labour and are burdened, and I will refresh you*" (Bk. IV, chap. 1, 2). The necessity for purity in one who approaches the sacrament is rightly stressed—more perhaps than would be thought necessary in a book written for the devout today—but he gives valuable advice about not putting off Holy Communion because of temptations, "For some people", he says, "when they set about preparing themselves for Holy Communion, are then subject to Satan's worst assaults . . . but no attention must be paid to his wiles and fancies" (Bk. IV, chap. 10, 2). So, too, a man may be hindered "by too great a solicitude for devotion, or by some anxiety or other about his confessions. But follow the counsel of the wise, and lay aside all anxiety and scruple; for these things hinder the grace of God and destroy the mind's devotion" (*ibid.,* 3). And throughout the work there is much sound and reassuring advice. The soul is not to be worried by a lack of feelings of devotion. "All is not therefore lost, if sometimes you have not that feeling towards me or my saints which you would like to have. . . . You ought not to lean too much upon it, because it comes and goes. But to fight against the evil motions of the mind which come upon you, and to despise the suggestions of the devil, this is a sign of virtue and great merit" (Bk. III, chap. 6, 2). The same salutary teaching is repeated later in this Book (chap. 35). "If you seek rest in this life, how then will you come to rest everlasting? (2). Do you think to have spiritual consolations always, whenever you please? My saints had not so; they met with many troubles and various temptations, and great desolations. But they bore all with patience and trusted more in God than in themselves" (3). And finally the soul must never be dejected by its difficulties and failures. "My son, patience and humility in adversity please me more than much consolation and devotion in prosperity" (Bk. III, chap. 57, 1). "To the best of your ability, put the tribulation out of your heart; and if it have affected you, yet let it not cast you down, or long embarrass you" (*ibid.*, 2).

The *Imitation of Christ* is one of the great books of spirituality. Perhaps none has been so much used, both within and without the Church, in the last five hundred years. If some have found it rather depressing—"the wind is always in the East in that book" is a remark that has been made about it—it must be remembered that it reflects the circumstances of its origin. It is an invitation to the lukewarm and the indifferent to turn to God, a call to repentance, always an astringent experience as well as a consoling one. The lasting demand for the book shows that it is never inappropriate.

OTHER WRITINGS OF THOMAS à KEMPIS

But the *devotio moderna* knew another aspect of the soul's relation with God. Whether or not Thomas à Kempis was the author of the *Imitation*, and it seems almost certain he was responsible for it in the form we know, he was certainly the author of a considerable body of writings. They consist of a number of sermons, and short works on the spiritual life (six volumes of the standard edition)[4] together with a history of Gerard Groot and his early disciples, and a life of St Lidwine of Schiedam. His spiritual works are all written very much in the style of the *Imitation*, in the form of simple counsels or *sententiae*. For the most part they would be described as ascetic rather than mystical, and their aim is to produce the simple, devout religious, the model for the older Orders which

[4] *Opera Omnia Thomae Hemerken à Kempis*, edit. Pohl, I–VIII (Fribourg, 1902–18).

was being set by the Brethren of the Common Life. But in some of these works he rises naturally and easily to what might be the outcome of such a life. Thus in the *Soliloquy of the Soul*[5] he begins with the fear of judgement and urges the soul to grieve and weep for its sins in accordance with the spirit of the reform, but the thought of the love of God and of the soul's union with him becomes more and more the theme.

> There shall be no fear, but love shall fill all, and trembling shall cease; for this change is of the right hand of God (chap. XI, 5). It is clear as day that the soul may be closely united to God by grace imparted unto it from heaven. Though it is a rare case, yet it is very dear and known to the loving soul. Difficult though it be, it is not altogether impossible. The soul that God shall so join to himself let none dare separate or disturb. If thou art astonished at the greatness of this union, be confounded and admire the excellence of his goodness, and the singular union in the assumption of humanity. (chap. XIII, 2.)

Thomas à Kempis lays as much stress on the fleeting nature of the experience of contemplation as the early medieval writers did. "Thou suddenly withdrawest from its hands when it thinketh not" (chap. XIII, 5). The withdrawal of contemplation causes grief and tribulation (XIV), but always in this latter part of the treatise the idea recurs of Christ's love for the soul (chap. XV, 3–9). He seems to withdraw himself, but "that it might be tried how true, strong, and chaste the power of love was, it was needful for temptation to manifest it. But I could not be tempted unless he permitted it, and withdrew himself for a season" (chap. XVI, 1). Characteristic of this stage of the soul's relation with God is the recognition that he does not desert it. "How great hath his mercy been towards me in that even when I knew and perceived it not, he was with me in trial" (*ibid.*, 4). Essentially his teaching is the same as that of the early medieval writers. The sincere desire

[5] *The Soliloquy of the Soul and the Garden of Roses*, by Thomas à Kempis. Translated by the Rev. W. B. Flower (London, 1853).

for God will result in finding him, and the soul will be conscious that it has done so in a very special way, but there is a complete absence of speculation on the nature of the union that may be implied. Just once there is recognition of the fact that it may be without any bodily image. "My God, when thou enterest into the soul that loves thee, wilt thou not feed it with milk, and of thy great sweetness lead it out of itself, to embrace thee without any bodily image?" (chap. X, 8). The Dionysian teaching was well known and it fitted the facts, but it is not made the object of constant effort. "The wind bloweth where it listeth", and there is to be no forcible striving after mystical union (cf. chap. XIII, 2 above). That this represented a reaction against the extreme speculative school is obvious, but it should be remembered that Ruysbroeck, at any rate, was held in great veneration by the Brethren of the Common Life. The early members had known him personally and revered his evident sanctity but, if their writings reflect at times parts of his teaching, fundamentally their approach to spirituality is different. They were not primarily interested in the higher forms of contemplation, but rather in introducing the sort of spirituality which St Francis de Sales later inculcated in his *Introduction to the Devout Life*, but it is to be noted that they were writing for religious rather than lay-folk.

GERSON

John Gerson (1363–1429) was an important figure in the troubled ecclesiastical politics of his time, but with that side of his activities we are not here concerned. Chancellor of the University of Paris, he was driven out by the Duke of Burgundy, John the Fearless, in 1418, and took refuge first at the Benedictine abbey of Melk in Austria, and later at Lyons where he died. He is an interesting and in many ways an attractive figure, who has left a large body of writings covering a wide range of subjects. As a dogmatic theologian he has run into some trouble for his views on papal supremacy, views prompted solely by the desire to bring the disastrous schism in the papacy to an end, but he has also left a considerable number of occasional tracts on various points of moral theology. They contain much valuable practical teaching, but fundamentally his moral theology is vitiated by the false principle, deriving ultimately from Occam, that the goodness or badness of an act depends on the arbitrary will of God. If his work in these fields reflects the political conditions and the intellectual influences of his century, his spiritual writings are representative of his time in so far as they show a return to the tradition of the early Middle Ages combined with certain features that were to be developed in the age that came after him. Born while Ruysbroeck was still alive, it was inevitable that he should have been interested speculatively in the problem of contemplation, and he made a study of it in his *Mystical Theology*.[6] The book consists of two parts which he calls speculative and practical. In the speculative part for the highest union of the soul with God he posited a higher intellect, the simple intelligence as he called it, and a superior appetite, synderesis, in the will. The acts proper to these powers were contemplation and ecstatic love, and the effect of this love is to absorb the soul, to unite it with God, and to give it complete satisfaction. This was in fact a scholastic exposition—it is largely based on St Bonaventure—of the Augustinian theory. Bonaventure at the end of the *Itinerarium mentis ad Deum* declined to go any further in defining the union, but since his day the German mystical school had gone to great lengths in doing so, and Gerson had already criticized a part of Ruysbroeck's *Spiritual Espousals*[7] for using terms which seem to imply that the soul becomes merged in God in some pantheistic sense. Here, in the *Mystical Theology*, he brings forward a number of theories

[6] *Opera Omnia* (Antwerp, 1706), III, col. 361. References are to this edition.
[7] *Opera Omnia*, I, col. 59.

which had been produced to account for the union only to reject them; he himself puts forward the view that it was a union of love, but he does not enlarge on it. In laying this stress on love, however, he was touching on an important point, for it is this which necessarily informs all Christian mysticism, and which marks the difference between the Greek and the Christian conception of contemplation. For the Greeks what was aimed at was the intellectual contemplation of the One, for the Christians it was union with a personal God. Whatever may be thought of Augustine's own contemplation, and there are those who think it was almost entirely intellectual, there can be no doubt of the part which love played in the spiritual writings of the Middle Ages which owed their inspiration ultimately to him. Gallus introduced it in his commentaries on pseudo-Denis, and the scholastic theologians brought out its significance. The thing known can only be known according to the capacity of the knower, but love is a going out and can go beyond the lover to something only dimly apprehended. Bonaventure saw that the intellect too, with divine help, must be transcended, and Gerson speaking of "perfect prayer"—using the word in the modern sense (see p. 125 below)—says that it "transcends both the mind and the spirit",[8] but he was frightened of a purely intellectual contemplation because of its pantheistic implications and preferred to lay the stress on love. Interestingly enough he later came round to the Dionysian view. In what is little more than a fragment[9] he discusses contemplation and says that many hold that it is a question of communication of knowledge, while others say that the affections play a larger rôle and that with the action of synderesis (as used by him) all intellectual participation must cease. He says that once he accepted this view himself thinking that it was that of Bonaventure and of those who commented on Denis. Now he thinks that in mystical theology (contemplation) neither will nor intellect—acting naturally—play any part. "When

[8] *Ibid.*, III, 397.   [9] *Ibid.*, I, 115.

the soul itself has been purified, simplified, and freed from all solicitude, all desire and all imagining, then mystical theology exists." But this is Gerson the academic theologian. It is one side of him; he had not risen to be Chancellor of the University of Paris for nothing, and he shows all the easy mastery of terms, and distinctions, and varying points of view, that we associate with the highly trained scholastic theologian. But there was always another side to Gerson. He was immensely practical, and zealous to use his learning for the immediate good of the Church or of individual souls. His *Mount of Contemplation* illustrates this well, but before going on to it we may note one other point that emerges from the practical part of his *Mystical Theology*, namely that a man should consider very carefully whether in fact he has a vocation to a life of contemplation—it being presupposed that he is addressing those dedicated in an especial way to the service of God. Not everyone, he says, has such a vocation. This is of great significance. The idea was not altogether new for he himself in *The Mount of Contemplation* quotes St Gregory to the same effect, but the fact remains that it was not a subject which preoccupied the early school. They sought God, and the degree of union which they might attain was ultimately his secret. In stressing the necessity for a temperamental aptitude Gerson was laying the foundations for the esoteric view of contemplation that was to hold sway until our own times, but which today is beginning to be queried in some quarters. The subject cannot be discussed here, but it would seem that the life of full contemplative union as it later came to be envisaged can only be for the very few and chosen souls to whom it is given.

The Mount of Contemplation[10] was originally written in French for some nuns, and the treatise shows signs of having been written, perhaps hastily, in answer to a particular demand. It is of interest, because in it we see his practical

[10] *Ibid.*, III, 545.

approach to the spiritual life. He uses the word contemplation in a wide sense. What the contemplative has to aspire after is the love of God, and when this reaches a sufficient degree of intensity it will absorb the soul in a manner analogous to the way in which any intense human interest will absorb it (chap. XX), and this in itself is at least the beginning of contemplation. The means to bring this about is meditation, and we can learn what he meant by this from a separate little treatise he wrote on the subject, *A Consoling treatise on Meditation*. He distinguishes it from what he calls mere thought (*cogitatio*) in two ways. It is in the first place controlled and concentrated, and *meditatio* may be compared to *cogitatio*, as writing to mere scribbling or doodling. But *meditatio* also implies that the affections are in some way engaged, a certain enthusiasm is engendered. There must be the *desire* of the earlier writers.

It is clear that the approach to contemplation that he here inculcates is substantially that of the early Middle Ages, and he does in fact refer in a rather summary way to a number of writers of that period, and recommends the prayers of St Anselm as a means of stimulating the sort of meditation he has in mind. The teaching is very characteristic of Gerson. Fundamentally he is basing himself on the pre-scholastic tradition, which in itself is further evidence for the fact that this tradition was never lost sight of, but he was also looking forward to a conception of meditation which would be developed after his time. This was the idea of meditation precisely as concentrated thought on a particular spiritual subject, but thought which was not just intellectual speculation, but was calculated to arouse the affections. The outcome, of course, would be affective prayer, and this no doubt was what had always been achieved in the meditative reading which the early Middle Ages knew as *lectio divina*. In Gerson we find the process more fully analysed than it had been previously, but not as clearly as it would be later. He realized

what the effects might be. Chapter XXXI tells how the contemplative soul is elevated above the body, and is made simple
and one. But with the earlier writers the line between meditation and contemplation is not drawn definitively. The one
process merges into the other. The point of interest here is
that this method of arriving at contemplation is quite distinct
from and incompatible with the Dionysian method as set
forth, for example, by the author of the *Cloud of Unknowing*.

The matter of false mysticism, which was still rife in the
Rhineland and Low Countries of his day, exercised him a
good deal, and he wrote two treatises on it apart from his
criticism of the *Spiritual Espousals, The Proving of Spirits*,[11]
and *The distinction between true and false visions*.[12] The
particular circumstances which were the immediate cause of
these writings would pass—though the question of the false
mystic remained a burning one for a long time and flared up
again in the seventeenth century. The significance of Gerson's
work on the subject was that it drew attention to the psycho-
physical aspects of mysticism and made them a part of the
subject, or if that is laying too much stress on the influence
of these writings, it would at least be true to say that he
showed the way in considering them as necessarily connected
with it. The theologians, of course, had considered the matter
long before,[13] and we have met these phenomena in the
German women mystics of the thirteenth century,[14] but the
writers who give instruction on spirituality right up to this
period ignore them. From now on at least the possibility of
their occurring in the higher reaches of the spiritual life has
to be taken into account as a matter of course.

---

[11] *Ibid.*, I, 37.
[12] *Ibid.*, I, 43.
[13] Cf. St Thomas, *Summa*, IIa, IIae, 174 and 176.
[14] The visions which appear plentifully in the works of the hagio-
graphers present a rather different problem. They are more in the
nature of *gratiae gratis datae*, and may be considered perhaps as part
of the problem presented by the proliferation of miracles in some of
these works. See *St Odo of Cluny*, Life by John of Salerno, translated
by Dom Gerard Sitwell (London, 1958), Introduction, pp. xviii ff.

DENIS THE CARTHUSIAN

Denis the Carthusian (1402–71) was a native of the Low Countries; he went through the schools at Cologne before becoming a Carthusian at the age of twenty-one. He was a strange and interesting figure. Notable as both an ascetic and a mystic—he is said to have had frequent ecstasies—he was also theologian, philosopher, commentator on Scripture and the writer of a number of treatises on the spiritual life. Indeed he must be among the most prolific writers of all time, and the modern edition of his works runs to forty-two volumes.[15] More erudite than original, he summarized the learning of the Middle Ages on all the subjects he touched, but although he rarely emerged from his Carthusian cell, he was well aware of the needs of the Church in his time, and particularly of the fundamental need for improving the standard of religious practice among both clergy and laity. For this purpose he wrote a number of treatises addressed to particular classes, and he is surprisingly minute in the objects of his attention.[16] Every section of the clergy from bishops to novices in religious Orders is considered, and among the laity, princes, the nobility, soldiers, merchants, judges, married people, widows, even Franciscan Tertiaries, all have a special treatise. There can be no question of examining all these in detail here, but we may note a few points. His purpose was to turn men and women whose adherence to the Catholic faith was little more than nominal into devout Christians, and his effort was part of that very real movement for reform from below which marked the fifteenth century and which, had it been more widespread and far-reaching, might have obviated the need for that cataclysm in the next century which goes by the name of the Reformation. The nature of the advice he gives is often very revealing. Thus, when he is addressing bishops, he urges them to find time for saying the divine Office fittingly,

[15] *Opera omnia* (Montreuil-sur-Mer and Tournai, 1896–1913). References are to this edition.
[16] These treatises are to be found in vols. xxxvii and xxxviii.

and not to say it hurriedly in a hole-and-corner manner. He impresses upon them the need for patience and constancy, and he exhorts them not to give benefices to unworthy recipients. On this particular abuse, which was rife in the Church at the time, he has indeed a special treatise. Bishops, he says, ought to say Mass at least sometimes. He devotes a special treatise to archdeacons, in whose hands much of the administration of the Church rested, and the width of his learning is shown in the knowledge of the law and of the principles which should govern its application which he displays. His treatise for parish priests is particularly interesting, for he does not merely remind them of the dignity of the priesthood and of their personal obligation to lead good lives, but he devotes the greater part of the treatise to showing them how they are to carry out their further obligation of instructing their people. He goes through the Ten Commandments as matter for preaching, illustrates the sort of advice which should be given to married people, and gives much valuable advice to priests on the manner of hearing confessions. The treatise is very illuminating on the needs of the Church in the fifteenth century. We take it for granted that priests are taught these things in the seminary, but seminaries were introduced by the Council of Trent, and the need which they met is very well illustrated by the sort of things which Denis the Carthusian thought it useful to say to the priests of his time. He is positive and helpful in the advice that he gives. Thus he bases his treatise for princes on the principle *noblesse oblige*. The glory of high position is that it entails the obligation of doing good, and he shows how the life of a ruler must be governed by the cardinal virtues of prudence, justice, fortitude and temperance. He acknowledges and justifies the need for recreation. It is governed by the virtue of *eutrapelia*. Princesses he evidently expected to be more pious, and he encourages them and instructs them accordingly. He gives the obvious advice to certain classes, to merchants, for example, to be fair-dealing and honest, and to judges to be just and to avoid the law's delays. In his little treatise for soldiers it is inspiring to find him holding up the ideal of the Christian man-at-arms as the defender and upholder of the state, and not merely inveighing against the more obvious vices in which he may be tempted to indulge.

Much has been made of the intensity with which he lived his life,[17] the frequent revelations and ecstasies, ferocious asceticism, constant resolving of doubts, difficulties and questions of conscience, all of which seems certainly to have fallen to his lot, even confined as he mostly was to his Charterhouse. All men of the Middle Ages, and particularly no doubt the waning Middle Ages, felt more passionately, or at any rate displayed their passions more freely, than we do, and yet the impression conveyed by reading these treatises is far from being that of an unbalanced mind. If his exposition of moral precepts was abstract and general, that also was characteristic of the Middle Ages to which he essentially belongs, but in any case it could hardly have been otherwise, granted his terms of reference. But what is striking about these writings is the way in which the academic learning of the schools is leavened by sympathy and understanding. Even ascetic treatises of a more general nature, which from their titles might be expected to be more uncompromising, show this quality. Thus in the little work *On the Straight Way of Salvation*[18] he is mostly positive. He lays stress on the lightness of Christ's yoke and gives instruction on prayer. Only in the *Mirror of Lovers of the World*[19] does he appeal more strongly and openly to fear as a motive for reform. In all of them, of course, he takes for granted the absolute faith of his readers, and in this, a generation later than Gerson, he was no doubt by and large justified. The first generations of Protestants, after all, retained their faith in the basic doctrines of Christianity, and not least in the doctrine of hell.

[17] J. Huizinga, *The Waning of the Middle Ages* (London, 1924), p. 171.
[18] *Opera omnia*, XXXIX, p. 421.
[19] *Ibid.*, p. 485.

In the confident sweep of his learning Denis took in even his pseudo-namesake, and he has left commentaries on most of his writings, but it is in two other works, *The Fount of Light*[20] and *On Contemplation*[21] that he sets forth his views on contemplation and the contemplative life most fully. The teaching is the same in both works, but *On Contemplation* gives the fuller treatment. He was versed in all that the Middle Ages had to say upon the subject, and his exposition is really a synthesis of the medieval teaching. Some consideration of his work will, therefore, provide a useful opportunity for pulling together all that has been said, and of seeing more accurately wherein lies the difference between the two main schools of thought.

As the ground-plan of the soul's activity in seeking God it will be well to recall the fourfold division of reading, meditation, prayer and contemplation, a division well known throughout the Middle Ages and referred to by Denis himself. We have seen how for John of Fécamp and Peter of Celle reading was the foundation of the whole process. We have also seen that reading in this context cannot be divorced from meditation, it is essentially thoughtful, meditative reading, and meditation is, of course, an act of the intellect. In this context it means the intellectual consideration of the truths of religion. But it must also have another quality: it must be affective. That is, the will must be involved; there must be love. Denis makes the point expressly both in a special work he wrote on the subject, the *De meditatione*, and again when speaking of contemplation. For him, there was no hard and fast dividing line between one and the other. Meditation, he says, without affection is *informis*, naked and ineffectual, and speaking of contemplation he says that it is loving knowledge, *affectuosa cognitio*.[22] He goes on to speak of contemplation as theological wisdom, attributing it to the

[20] *Ibid.*, XLI, p. 91.
[21] *Ibid.*, p. 133.
[22] *De meditatione*, Proemium, XLI, p. 69.

gift of the Holy Ghost, and he distinguished it from philosophical wisdom which, he says, is *informis* and *nuda*.[23]
Hilton makes the same distinction. His first degree of contemplation is attained by reason only, and he says it may be called "a sort of contemplation inasmuch as it is a certain realization of truth" (Bk. I, chap. IV), but he adds that it is not real contemplation for it does not demand charity and may be attained by the good and the bad alike. The older writers, such as John of Fécamp, expressed the need for this affective quality of reading or meditation by saying that there must be desire for God. Always it is implied that there must be something positive about this. Their reading is informed by charity, but in a way which implies something more than the way in which any act of a person in a state of grace may be said to be informed by charity. The bringing of the will into action is, of course, prayer. The process may be compared to the modern exercise of mental prayer. In this there is first the action of the intellect finding motives for sorrow, or the love of God, or whatever it may be, and from this will follow acts of the will in which the prayer properly consists. Meditation, then, leads in the way with which we are familiar to prayer, but the medieval writers, and this is true of all of them, although they used this fourfold division of reading, meditation, prayer and contemplation, in fact hardly mention prayer, and they thought of it in the older sense as primarily petition. For us the transition is from reading to meditation, to prayer, and possibly to contemplation. For the medievals the transition was from reading to meditation and to contemplation. We use prayer in a wide sense which may include contemplation; they used contemplation in a wide sense which may include what we call affective prayer.

Denis throws more light on the medieval conception of contemplation by describing it in a number of different ways. He says that there are three stages on the way to contemplation, the purgative, illuminative and unitive. This is, of course,

[23] *De contemplatione*, I, 10.

the old division first formulated in these terms by Bonaventure. They were not used a great deal in the Middle Ages, though much since. The purgative way is the initial preparation always demanded, the overcoming of sin and the acquirement of virtue, Cassian's practical life. When he comes to the illuminative way, Denis says it means the "occupation of the mind in the contemplation of divine things, when it bends all its efforts to consider spiritual, supernatural and heavenly good by participation in the divine light, receiving the rays of supernatural wisdom, but created and infused. When it is illuminated by this light it sees the divine, and it is made the bride-chamber of the spouse . . . God instructs ît in all things with most sweet unction."[24] A little later he says

> When the soul has been reformed in this way in its sensitive appetite (the purgative way), and the mind has been adorned (the illuminative way), it is fit to enter the third way . . . where it is enflamed with vehement love from the contemplation of the divine; altogether on fire, it is made burning and alight, as though enkindled by the immense fire of the divinity through the falling on it of certain sparks.[25]

The soul transcends all created things and, forgetful of self and everything else, it is absorbed in God. Such is the way Denis speaks of the stages in the soul's union with God, using the metaphors of fire and light.

He then goes on to say[26] that contemplation is twofold. It may be through affirmation or negation. In *The Fount of Light* (12) he puts this more clearly by saying that there are two ways to God, through creatures and by abstracting from creatures. He refers to the pseudo-Denis as his authority for both. In the *Divine Names* this author says that everything can be affirmed of God in the sense that he contains all, but everything can be denied as applying to him, in as much as in himself he is incomprehensible to the created mind. In the *Mystical Theology* he teaches the way of negation with which his name is associated. The Carthusian does not enlarge very

[24] *De cont.*, I, 19. [25] *Ibid.*, I, 19. [26] *Ibid.*, I, 26.

much on the distinction he makes, but in *The Fount of Light* he says that the latter way, by abstraction, is the more sublime and perfect. The reference, however, would certainly seem to be to the two approaches we have been following. The way of negation is the way of Eckhart and the *Cloud of Unknowing*. All thought of every created thing must be beaten down and the mind concentrated on the simplest idea of God. The way of affirmation, through creatures, is precisely through meditation. And the humanity of Christ, it is to be remembered, is created. For Denis, there are two approaches and they are the ones we have been considering, leading to the same result.

Throughout the Middle Ages, then, it is recognized that reading may lead to meditation, and that thence the soul may be led to affective prayer and contemplation proper, though there is little analysis of contemplation and the two later stages are not distinguished. This is the old way, the way of affirmation in Denis's terminology. It would not, however, be true to say that the way of negation jumps straight to contemplation. The author of the *Cloud* is insistent that there must be much reading and meditation on the life of Christ before the soul can put itself to the exercise which he recommends, but the whole point of his treatise is that for a person at a certain stage of the spiritual life there must be a conscious and deliberate effort to attain contemplation directly through what may be called the negation technique. That is to say through the deliberate exclusion of all discursive thought, and the concentration of the mind on the simple idea of God. It might, and should perhaps, be said that strictly speaking this is not an effort to attain contemplation, which is recognized to be the free gift of God, but is rather putting oneself in a state which predisposes as far as is humanly possible for the gift. It is an attempt to remove all obstacles and to leave the soul open to the divine action. Denis is a good witness that both methods were known at the end of the Middle Ages. He is more impressed by the second, but his description of the ascent of the soul through the three ways rather suggests the former.

That is as far as the problem of contemplation was taken within the limits we have set ourselves for this little work.[27] At a later period a break was made in the old sequence, reading, meditation, prayer, contemplation. The relation between meditation and prayer was studied and developed. It was the birth of what we now call mental prayer. But at that stage a stop was put, and the ordinary person was not expected to go beyond it. Only the chosen soul under the strict guidance of a director might embark on the pursuit of contemplation, and this when it was done was by the method of negation. The process was called giving up meditation, and though it always had its exponents, the majority of directors for many centuries were very nervous about allowing souls to enter this stage. Psychologically no doubt the thing happens automatically; an affective, meditative prayer becomes more and more simplified in its intellectual content as it approaches contemplation. On the other hand, of course, the mere cessation of meditation does not ensure, still less does it constitute, contemplation. An elaborate scheme of the various spiritual states and degrees of prayer through which the soul might pass was evolved, but in practice each individual soul presents a state which is at once simpler and more subtle than anything which can be reflected in rigid categories. The result of this dichotomy among the devout between what came to be called the contemplative and non-contemplative state had undesirable effects in so far as it was apt to induce a sort of spiritual self-consciousness. There was danger of an undue desire or an undue fear of contemplative prayer. It was of course the fear of false mysticism, such as we have noted was

[27] The dispute which arose in the middle of the century about the so-called Learned Ignorance, *Ignorantia docta*, whether the intellect played any part at all in the attainment of union with God, was not important or far-reaching. The cardinal, Nicholas of Cusa, was the chief representative of the more moderate exponents of the anti-intellectualist position.

displayed by Gerson, which induced the hardening of this division of the spiritual life into two clear-cut departments; mental prayer for the many, contemplative prayer for the few. The Quietist controversy in France in the seventeenth century accentuated it, and only in our own day has a tendency manifested itself to regard contemplation as at least a possible and legitimate climax to any intensely led spiritual life.

SPIRITUAL EXERCISES

One last feature of fifteenth-century spirituality falls within the scope of this book. It manifested itself in two ways which were closely allied. One was the development of meditation and the other of Spiritual Exercises in the technical sense in which the expression came to be used. Both were the outcome of the widespread need which was felt for reform. It is worth recalling that John of Fécamp and the people he wrote for— and equally the early Cistercians—did not stand in need of reform in any comparable way. The spirituality of the early Middle Ages was a spirituality of the cloisters, and in the eleventh and twelfth centuries the life in these was inspired by a series of reforms beginning with that of Cluny. The inhabitants of the cloisters, by the mere fact that they were there, were marked out as a spiritual *élite*. By the end of the Middle Ages this was no longer so. But it was not merely that the standard had dropped, as it undoubtedly had in the older houses; the whole intellectual atmosphere had changed. In the early Middle Ages to turn to God wholeheartedly presented no doubt a moral problem for the individual, but hardly an intellectual one. There were some few sects which did not accept the Church's scheme of things, but they were in no way representative of society at large. For the ordinary man or woman the choice was clear, even if the decision was hard to make. With the coming of the Renaissance and humanism an intellectual problem was also posed. It was not only that there was a new paganism in the form of a revival of the old—few probably took this seriously—but a humanistic outlook had arisen to confront Christianity. It was the anthropocentric view of the world which is still with us. Very often, no doubt, it was, and is, a practical way of looking at life rather than a thought-out scheme, but it engendered a frame of mind which did not readily accept the Christian position. Hence the necessity for a change in the manner of meditation. There had always been meditation, as we have seen, but it had been the loving consideration of the truths of religion by a believer. Now something different was required, even if there was still room for the old as well. There was need for producing, or at any rate for strengthening, intellectual conviction. This was manifesting itself already in the fifteenth century and would do so more as the Renaissance gathered impetus and spread to the North, because for one thing the reading public among the laity was becoming considerable—in the earlier Middle Ages it hardly existed—and the layman was in need of conversion in a way that he had not been before. This need came to be appreciated and was later catered for, but if we examine the fifteenth-century books of meditation and spiritual exercises we find that they were meant for religious. The fact is very enlightening. How did it come that religious were in want of this sort of conviction? The answer reminds us of the change that was coming, or had come, over the religious Orders. People were entering them later in life from a world in which religious values were not taken for granted in the way they had been, and the founders of the new Orders, and those who were responsible for reforming the old, realized that their subjects were not likely to make a success of their lives unless these rested on a firm intellectual basis. Thus, in the following century, when the Jesuits were founded, the Jesuit novice was required to make an "election" in the long retreat at the beginning of his noviciate, even though he had in a sense made one by entering the noviciate at all.

MAUBURNUS

The instruction of the layman in the devout life was necessary if the internal reform of the Church was really going to be effective, but the needs of the religious Orders were as great in this matter and it was properly enough with these that the process began. We can see it in action very well in the writings of Mauburnus (Mombaer, † 1502). He is a particularly good witness because, a religious of the Congregation of Windesheim who had known Thomas à Kempis, he went to France, where he reformed a number of houses including the royal abbey of St Séverin and the abbey of the Canons Regular at Livry near Paris, and he has left us in a large work, the *Rosetum*,[28] a very full programme of the sort of instruction in the religious life on which he based his reform. The title, a *Rosary*, suggests the form of the work, which is in effect a vast collection of small treatises, which are however strung together on a plan. The book falls into two parts which expound the active and contemplative lives, but he interprets these terms in a very wide sense. The active, he says, is simply concerned with performance, the best way of doing things, the contemplative with meditation and the fullest understanding (p. 28). Into this division he works the now familiar distinctions of the purgative, illuminative and unitive ways. The purgative way corresponds to the active life, the illuminative to the contemplative, and the unitive is confined to a small subdivision at the end of this, and even then we find it does not introduce anything different from what has gone before. Although he says that meditation belongs to the second part, and he there elaborates his treatment of it, he prefaces the whole book with a disquisition on the subject. He begins by comparing it to mental prayer. As mental prayer is not perfunctory and superficial, not merely verbal or vocal, but internal, attentive and affective, so is the meditation of

[28] *Rosetum exercitiorum spiritualium* (Milan, 1603). References are to this edition.

which he will treat. It demands judgement on the things thought of and excites the desire for them. He mentions various objections which are brought against this meditation of which the only significant and the interesting one is that it is unusual, and accustomed exercises are not easily to be changed. The significance of this objection he later brings out when he states—and he quotes the authority of one James the Carthusian for his statement—that the failure of the religious Orders is due to the lack of initial training and instruction which their members receive (p. 29). In particular, he says, the religious are not instructed as novices in internal exercises of devotion and piety, but their practice remains superficial and external. He does not mince his words, but goes on to describe the inhabitants of the cloisters as animal and carnal, thinking that all they have to do to be saved is to wear the religious habit and be tonsured, to perform their ceremonies and to sing the canonical Hours (pp. 29, 30). This was, of course, the opinion of a reformer, and perhaps some exaggeration should be allowed for, but in the main the history of the religious houses at the time bears it out. The emphasis on the purely external character of current observances gives the clue to the nature of his own work.

The *Rosetum* is a long book and there is an intricate system of divisions and subdivisions, but the greater part of the first half is given up to a detailed description of how to sanctify the various actions of the day, and to a consideration of Holy Communion and the part it should play in the spiritual life. In the section called *Dietarium* (Journal) he goes through the whole monastic day discussing the significance of everything that has to be done and suggesting the proper dispositions in which to do it. Many pages are devoted to getting up for the night Office. Suitable texts to think of, to meditate upon, are supplied, remedies suggested against oversleeping, and so on. A lengthy paragraph is devoted to the sign of the cross, many more pages deal with the preparation that should be made in choir before beginning Matins.

Later he has a special section on the way of saying Office in choir in which he suggests pious thoughts for the most part meditation on the passion, to accompany the various Hours, but in the *Dietarium* he contents himself with general exhortations and warning against such failures as going to sleep. If any should be so unfortunate as to do this, they are to recall to mind when they wake up all the pains of hell, of which he gives a picturesque catalogue. This, as a matter of fact, is not characteristic of the tone. In general he aims at making the monk reflect on his duties throughout the day in order that he may realize how he is living his life in the service of God. There is wisdom and humanity in the book. He says, for example, that the weaker brethren should go to bed at once after Matins and should not make special devotions of their own.

That Mauburnus should have written at length on the Eucharist is interesting.[29] Today we should take it as natural that an important place in the spiritual life of a young religious should be given to the reception of Holy Communion, yet in the earlier Middle Ages we do not find it really integrated into the spiritual life of the monks. None of the authors whose works we have considered wrote a specific treatise on the subject or did more than make incidental reference to it. Mauburnus, however, says that not less attention is to be paid to it in the life of the religious than to the divine Office. He lays a good deal of stress—perhaps significantly—on the danger of making unworthy Communions, and sets out a scheme of eucharistic devotions for each day of the week. A large part of the section which he devotes to the Eucharist is given the subtitle *De ruminatione*. By this he means consideration of Holy Communion in all its aspects. Without this, he says, we shall not get the full effects from it. It is to be noted that under this heading he conveys a lot of instruction that would now be conveyed in the ordinary course of

---

[29] It is worth recalling that the whole of the fourth book of the *Imitation* is given up to the same subject.

theology pursued by any student for the priesthood; the reasons for going to Communion, the dispositions required, the fruits proper to the reception of the sacrament. He even discusses the more purely speculative question of the manner of Christ's presence—a reminder that the comprehensive course of theology we now take for granted was as yet unknown.

The second Part of the work he calls *Exercises of the contemplative life* and his treatment of the subject is most interesting. He devotes the whole part in one way or another to meditation. In the Introduction to the whole work he made it clear that he advocates meditation in the broad sense that behind the performance of all the duties of the life of the cloister there must lie a realization of what it is the religious is really doing. There must be a constant effort to turn the whole life into the service of God, and not to allow it to become a routine accepted through custom, the purpose of which is not properly understood or adverted to. Now in a section headed *Meditatorium* he goes on to speak of meditation in a more particularized sense. He says that he does not wish to treat of sublime things and to explain the matter of contemplation, but only to discuss the affective meditation of simple souls (*rudi*) for, he says, this will more quickly lead to the citadel of mystical theology than if he were to hold forth on sublime and deep matters (p. 412). He has no wish to distinguish between contemplation, meditation and thought, he says, for there are many other books on these subjects, but it befits him to labour at giving practical advice. He goes at considerable length into this affective meditation, composing a ladder of meditation which has no less than twenty-three rungs. But throughout the process is what we mean by meditation, thought leading to affection, and finally complete resignation of self-will to the will of God (pp. 420–7).

We may note two things about all this. Firstly, it is obvious that affective meditation is prayer. The third term of the medieval sequence: reading, meditation, prayer, contemplation, has been given its full value. He states expressly that the prayer may become contemplative, may lead to the citadel of mystical theology. This is exactly what we have described as the approach to the spiritual life of the early Middle Ages. Secondly, he says that he will not speak of contemplation directly, and he is true to his word, for, long as his ladder is, it stops short of contemplation proper. In refraining from introducing contemplation into his actual scheme, in spite of what he had said just before, he illustrates very well the reaction against the speculative mysticism of Eckhart and Ruysbroeck which was characteristic of the Brethren of the Common Life to whom he belonged. He is very much more explicit about the nature of meditation than the earlier writers had been, but he did not reduce it to the art which it would later become. There is nothing about set periods, though these would surely seem to be implied, nor about points in the way in which these were later understood, though he does say, when acknowledging the difficulty of putting his teaching into practice, that it is well to make a collection of points for meditation on chosen topics, and to add to it as time goes on (p. 416). The idea, which he took from Gerson, seems to be to have something to fall back on, but he is not very explicit on this. It was a subject which would be highly developed later. Nevertheless he does take up the question of prayer and contemplation again in another context and refers explicitly to St Bernard's sequence of reading, meditation, prayer and contemplation (p. 417). In a great quantity of not very well ordered matter we may just note two further points. He recognizes that aridity will be experienced, and he stresses the fact that to learn the art of meditating will take effort and time. And rather interestingly he says in a note that we should try to meditate without phantasms. Much of the matter that he proposes, the life and passion of Christ and God's benefits to us, clearly do not allow of this. But he makes the statement out of deference to authorities, and he remarks that many have suggested many methods of doing it. But, he says, after the grace of God the most efficacious means in the opinion of a certain doctor is a vehement love for God, for it can hardly be that one who sincerely loves God alone will think of him with difficulty, and his meditation will become stabilized. And, because love breaks out more and more in acts the more closely the matter under consideration is examined, the cultivation of love will free the mind from phantasms. The certain doctor is, of course, Gerson, whom he mentions by name a little later. The significance of Gerson's emphasis on love has been pointed out,[30] but it hardly amounted to positive instruction about the *via negativa*. It was mentioned that Mauburnus only assigned one section of this part to the unitive way. The *Inflammatorium* he calls it, "To enflame love", and it only extends what he has already said by giving further *reasons* for loving God. It is just supplying further matter for meditation.

This is what Mauburnus had to offer to the monasteries that he reformed in France, and it is evidently, as we might expect, the spirituality of the *Imitation of Christ* applied in detail to the life of the cloister. It is a severely practical spirituality whose aim is first to give internal significance to the outward actions of the religious life, and secondly, closely connected with this but adding something to it, to inculcate the methodical practice of prayer.

GARCIA DE CISNEROS

While this reform of the religious life was being carried out by the Congregation of Windesheim, a similar reform was being initiated apparently quite independently by Louis Barbo († 1443), abbot of the Benedictine monastery of St Justina at Padua. The basis of Barbo's method was also the use of meditation, and he himself wrote a *Method of Meditation*, which outlined a brief course and provided a collection of meditations which might be used. Barbo himself did not

[30] *Supra*, p. 117.

visit Spain but his reform was conveyed, seemingly very effectively, to the Congregation of Valladolid by letter, and from Valladolid Garcia de Cisneros set out in 1492 to reform the abbey of Montserrat. There he wrote his *Exercises*,[31] which were printed at Montserrat in 1500 and may thus be said to come just within our purview. The book contained a scheme of meditations to be spread over three weeks. The first week is devoted to subjects suitable to the purgative way, sin, death, hell, etc., with a view to exciting sentiments of fear and contrition. The meditations of the second week aim at exciting the love of God in the soul. This is the illuminative stage where the soul is enlightened on the supernatural realities. In the third week, which embraces the unitive way, the soul unites itself in love with God. Here we have for the first time a system of Exercises. In the *Rosetum* Mauburnus had demonstrated a way of sanctifying the religious life in which the practice of meditation played an essential part. It did so because the necessary concomitant of his meditation was prayer of one degree or another—the two were interdependent—and prayer is essentially the expression of some sort of union with God, and is therefore the vital sap of the spiritual life. It had always been so of course, and Mauburnus only differed from his predecessors in this, that in the conditions of his day he found it necessary to be more explicit about the need, and to provide instruction in its practice.

The *Exercises* of Cisneros provided something rather different. They constituted a course carefully adapted to the varying characteristics of the Three Ways, and the serious following of them was calculated to provide something more than a merely superficial or theoretical acquaintance with the whole gamut of the spiritual life. It is not quite clear just how often this course was to be taken. Certainly it began the religious life, and at Montserrat in the early days of the

[31] They have been printed in English. *A Book of Spiritual Exercises and a Directory for the Canonical Hours* by Garcia de Cisneros. Translated by a monk of St Augustine's, Monastery, Ramsgate (London, 1876).

reform the monks were apparently made to learn the *Exercises* by heart[32] and were not allowed to read anything else till they had mastered them. In order to achieve its full effect a course of the Exercises would evidently have to be followed up, and the habitual practice of meditation, which was as much a feature of Barbo's reform as of the other, would provide the opportunity. A quarter of a century later St Ignatius was to produce the classic form of such a course of exercises. Whether the *Exercises* of Cisneros are to be regarded as in any sense a direct source for the Ignatian Exercises is immaterial—it would seem that little or nothing was borrowed direct. But Cisneros had launched something new in the spiritual life. He gave the primitive form to an instrument which Ignatius would perfect, and he inaugurated something which at least in the form of an annual retreat has become standard practice in religious Orders.

One other feature of the *Exercises* of Cisneros should be noted. After laying down his course of meditations, he devotes more than half his book—which is much shorter than the *Rosetum*—to the subject of contemplation. It is interesting that the Benedictine should have done this when Mauburnus declined to give any separate treatment to the subject. It can be said quite simply that Cisneros in his treatment of contemplation in this section of his work goes back to the tradition of the early Middle Ages, and ignores the Dionysian tradition altogether. He sees contemplation as always arising out of meditation.

An attempt has been made to distinguish two schools of thought about the contemplative life. Obviously they have much in common. They share an introductory training in the practice of fundamental virtue—which demands, of course, a continued effort—and they both presuppose a devotion to Christ nourished by meditation on his life and passion. The ultimate achievement when it is reached is the same. If the lines leading from the beginning to the end of the course tend

[33] *Revue Bénédictine*, XVII, p. 369.

to blend and merge at intervals, it remains true that there was a difference in attitude sufficiently fundamental to make the distinction beween the two schools of thought valid, and this will appear the more so if it be remembered that behind the one lies the conception of theology held by the Greek theologians, and behind the other the Neo-Platonist conception of the contemplative life.

It may be that the idea of a purely contemplative life in the sense envisaged by Cassian, in which the attempt is made to achieve an almost literally continuous concentration of the mind on God, came, through Greek philosophy, from the East. At any rate it is an idea which is still at home there in a way that it has never been in the West. At a very early date before the Christian era a system of conditioning the body to enable it to lead such a life had been developed in India (yoga), and perhaps this is necessary for its successful attainment. In the first part of our period the life led by the Cistercians and Carthusians was not contemplative in this sense. It was a life wholly devoted to the service of God, to which the actual practice of contemplation was strictly incidental. For the Eckhart and Ruysbroeck school its attainment was not incidental. They inaugurated in the West what can only be called a cult of contemplation. This was not accepted quite easily, on the contrary it aroused considerable alarm, but after the first reaction the effects of the interest in contemplation for itself, and a deepened appreciation of it which owed much to the German mystics, continued to be felt, but now it came to be exercised only under carefully controlled conditions.

This study of spirituality in the Middle Ages has been confined to the lands north of the Alps, because it was there that the theory was most discussed and the greatest amount of practical instruction provided. Spain, whose influence was to be predominant in the sixteenth century, had only just succeeded by the end of our period in throwing off the yoke of the Moors. Italy in the Middle Ages produced a number of women saints who were ecstatics and mystics, St Angela of Foligno († 1309), and the three St Catherines, of Siena († 1380), Bologna († 1463) and Genoa († 1510), but great as they were a study of them hardly belongs to a work such as this. They transcended schools and had each her own intensely personal message to convey. It might be argued that the message of Julian of Norwich was no less personal, and indeed she conforms to the pattern of these great women saints, but, though she is on a lesser scale than any of them, she seemed worth including because she belongs to the little English group, which as a whole comes naturally into the picture. In the person of St Laurence Justinian Italy did indeed provide one figure who was representative of traditional spirituality. The contemporary of Gerson, his works afford a striking parallel, but he was less academic, and apparently untouched by the Rhineland mystics.

SELECT BIBLIOGRAPHY

In this series: PALANQUE, J. R.: *The Church and the Dark Ages* (American edn, *The Dawn of the Middle Ages*); GUILLEMAIN, Bernard: *The Early Middle Ages* and *The Later Middle Ages*.

AELRED, St: *St Aelred's Letter to his Sister*, edited and translated by Geoffrey Webb and Adrian Walker, London, Mowbray, 1957; *On Jesus at Twelve Years Old*, Meditations of St Aelred translated from the Latin by Geoffrey Webb and Adrian Walker, London, Mowbray, 1956.

ANSELM, St: *Prayers and Meditations*, edited and translated by a Religious C.S.M.V., London, Mowbray, 1952.

ARTHUR, J. P. (translator): *The Chronicle of the Canons Regular of Mount Saint Agnes*, London, Kegan Paul, 1906.

BAZIRE, Joyce, and COLLEDGE, Eric (Editors): *The Chastising of God's Children and the Treatise of Perfection of the Sons of God*, Oxford, Blackwell, 1957.

BENEDICT, St: *The Rule* in Latin and English, edited and translated by Justin McCann, London, Burns & Oates, and Westminster, Md, Newman Press, 1952.

BERNARD, St: *On the Love of God*, translated with notes by T. L. Connolly, London, Burns & Oates, 1937; *Of Conversion*, text with translation and notes by Watkin Williams, London, Burns & Oates, 1938; *The Twelve Degrees of Humility and Pride*, translated by B. R. V. Mills, London, S.P.C.K., 1929; *Concerning Grace and Free Will*, translated by Watkin Williams, London, S.P.C.K., 1920; *The Letters of St Bernard of Clairvaux*, translated by Bruno S. James, London, Burns & Oates, and Chicago, Regnery, 1953; *Selections of Sermons on the Christian Year*, translated by a Religious C.S.M.V., London, Mowbray, and New York, Morehouse, 1954; *Sermons on the Song of Songs*, translated by S. J. Eales in *Life and Works of St Bernard*, Volume IV, London, John Hodges, 1896; *On the Song of Songs*, translated by a Religious C.S.M.V., London, Mowbray, and New York, Morehouse, 1952.

BONAVENTURE, St: *Meditations on the Life of Christ*, attributed to St Bonaventure, translated by Sr Emmanuel, O.S.B., St Louis and London, Herder, 1934; *Three Treatises on the Religious Life*, translated by Dominic Devas, O.F.M., London, Thomas Baker, 1922; *Breviloquium*, translated by E. E. Nemmers, St Louis and London, Herder, 1946.

BOUYER, Louis: *The Cistercian Heritage*, London, Mowbray, 1958.

BROWNE, Carleton: *Religious Lyrics of the XIIIth Century*, London and New York, Oxford Univ. Press, 1932; *Religious Lyrics of the XIVth Century*, London and New York, Oxford Univ. Press, 1924 (revised edn, 1952); *Religious Lyrics of the XVth Century*, London and New York, Oxford Univ. Press, 1939.

CASSIAN, John: *Institutes* and *Conferences*, Volume XI, Library of Nicene and Post-Nicene Fathers, Oxford, Parker, and New York, Christian Literature Co., 1894.

CHADWICK, O.: *John Cassian*, Cambridge and New York, Cambridge Univ. Press, 1950.

CLARK, J. M.: *The Great German Mystics*, Oxford, Blackwell, 1949.

DANIEL, Walter: *The Life of Aelred of Rievaulx*, translated with Introd. and Notes by F. M. Powicke, London, Nelson, and New York, Oxford Univ. Press, 1950.

DANIÉLOU, Jean, S.J.: *Origen*, translated by W. Mitchell, London and New York, Sheed and Ward, 1955.

ECKHART, Meister: *Meister Eckhart, Selected Writings*, translated and edited by James M. Clark and John V. Skinner, London, Faber, and New York, Nelson, 1958.

GARCIA DE CISNEROS: *A Book of Spiritual Exercises and a Directory for the Canonical Hours*, translated by a Monk of St Augustine's Abbey, Ramsgate, London, Burns & Oates, 1876.

GARDNER, Edmund: *The Cell of Self-Knowledge*, seven early English mystical treatises, London, Chatto and Windus, 1910.

GERSON, John: *John Gerson, Reformer and Mystic*, by James L. Connolly, Louvain, Librairie Universitaire, 1928.

GILSON, E.: *The Mystical Theology of St Bernard*, translated by A. H. C. Downes, London and New York, Sheed and Ward, 1940.

GRAEF, Hilda: *The Light and the Rainbow*, London, Longmans, and Westminster, Md, Newman Press, 1959.

GUY, II, Ninth Prior of Grande Chartreuse: *A Ladder of Four Rungs*, edited by Justin McCann, Stanbrook, 1953.

HILTON, Walter: *The Scale of Perfection*, ed. E. Underhill, 1923, reprint 1950, London, John Watkins; translated into modern English with Introduction and Notes by G. Sitwell, London, Burns & Oates, 1953, and Westminster, Md, Newman Press, 1954; *Minor Works*, edited by D. Jones, London, Burns & Oates, 1929; *Of Angels' Song and Epistle on Mixed Life* in *Richard Rolle and his Followers* edited by C. Horstman, Volume I, London, Swan, Sonnenschein, 1895.

HODGSON, P.: *The Cloud of Unknowing and the Book of Privy Counselling*, edited for E.E.T.S., London, 1944, reprint with additions, 1958.

HUIZINGA, J.: *The Waning of the Middle Ages*, London, Arnold, 1924.

JULIAN OF NORWICH: *Revelations of Divine Love*, edited by R. Hudleston, London, Burns & Oates, 1927 (reprint, · 1952), and Westminster, Md, Newman Press, 1952; the shorter version: *A Shewing of God's Love*, edited by A. M. Reynolds, London and New York, Longmans, 1958.

KEMPE, Margery: *The Book of Margery Kempe*, edited by S. B. Meech and H. E. Allen, E.E.T.S. (original series 112), London, 1940; a modern version by W. Butler-Bowdon, London, Cape, 1936.

KNOWLES, M. D.: *The Monastic Order in England*, Cambridge and New York, Cambridge Univ. Press, 1940; *The Religious Orders in England*, 3 volumes, Cambridge and New York, Cambridge Univ. Press, 1948–59; *The English Mystical Tradition*, London, Burns & Oates, and New York, Harper, 1961.

McCANN, J.: *The Cloud of Unknowing and other Treatises*, London, Burns & Oates, and Westminster, Md, Newman Press, revised edn 1952.

MOLINARI, Paul: *Julian of Norwich*, London, Longmans, 1958.

PETER DAMIAN, St: *Selected Writings on the Spiritual Life*, translated with an Introduction by Patricia McNulty, London, Faber, 1959.

POURRAT, Pierre: *Christian Spirituality*, volumes I–III, London, Burns & Oates, 1922–7; volumes I–IV, Westminster, Md, Newman Press, 1953–8.

ROLLE, Richard: *Richard Rolle, English Writings*, edited by Hope Emily Allen, London, Oxford Univ. Press, 1931. (This is a critical text containing the *Epistles* and a selection from the other writings); *The Fire of Love and Mending of Life*, translated in 1434 by Richard Misyn,.edited and done into modern English by F. M. Comper, London, Methuen, 1920 (2nd edn); *Selected Works* by G. C. Heseltine, London, Longmans, 1930 (Versions in modern English of the Epistles and some Scripture commentaries, with a translation of the *Emendatio*).

RUYSBROEK, J.: *Jan van Ruysbroek, the Spiritual Espousals*, translated from the Dutch with an Introduction by Eric Colledge, London, Faber, 1952; *The Seven Steps of the Ladder of Spiritual Love*, translated from the Flemish by F. Sherwood Taylor, London, Dacre Press, and Naperville, Ill., Allenson, 1952.

Suso, Henry: *The Little Book of Eternal Wisdom and the Little Book of Truth*, translated with Introduction and Notes by James M. Clark, London, Faber, and New York, Harper, 1953; *The Life of the Servant*, translated by James M. Clark, London, Faber, and Naperville, Ill., Allenson, 1952.

Tauler, John: *The History and Life of the Revd Dr John Tauler of Strasbourg*, by S. Winkworth, London, Smith Elder, 1857 (contains translations of a number of sermons, though not all are authentic); *Signposts to Perfection, a Selection of the Sermons of J. Tauler*, selected and translated by E. Strakosch, London, Blackfriars, 1958.

Thomas à Kempis: *The Soliloquy of the Soul and the Garden of Roses*, translated by W. B. Flower, London, Masters, 1853; *Imitation*, translated Justin McCann, London, Burns & Oates, and Westminster, Md, Newman Press, 1952; many other edns.

William of St Thierry: *The Epistle to the Brethren of Mont Dieu*, translated by Walter Shewring and edited by Justin McCann, London, Sheed and Ward, 1930; *The Mirror of Faith*, translated by Geoffrey Webb and Adrian Walker, London, Mowbray, 1959; *On Contemplating God*, translated by Geoffrey Webb and Adrian Walker, London, Mowbray, 1955; *On the Nature and Dignity of Love*, translated by Geoffrey Webb and Adrian Walker, London, Mowbray, 1956; *The Meditations of William of St Thierry*, translated by a Religious of C.S.M.V., London, Mowbray, 1954.